# Educating Rita

A comedy

# Willy Russell

Samuel French — London
New York - Toronto - Hollywood

*EDUCATING RITA* is fully protected under the copyright laws of the British Commonwealth, including Canada, the United States of America, and all other countries of the Copyright Union. All rights, including professional and amateur stage productions, recitation, lecturing, public reading, motion picture, radio broadcasting, television and the rights of translation into foreign languages are strictly reserved.

ISBN 978-0-573-11115-0

www.samuelfrench-london.co.uk

www.samuelfrench.com

---

### FOR AMATEUR PRODUCTION ENQUIRIES

### UNITED KINGDOM AND WORLD
### EXCLUDING NORTH AMERICA
plays@SamuelFrench-London.co.uk
020 7255 4302/01

Each title is subject to availability from Samuel French,

depending upon country of performance.

---

# EDUCATING RITA

First produced at The Warehouse, London, by the Royal Shakespeare Company, June 10th, 1980, and subsequently at the Piccadilly Theatre with the following cast of characters:

| | |
|---|---|
| **Frank** | Mark Kingston |
| **Rita** | Julie Walters |

Directed by Mike Ockrent
Designed by Poppy Mitchell

The action takes place in a first-floor room in a university in the north of England

Time—the present

**Author's Note to the revised edition of *Educating Rita***

Whilst I realise that the text of *Educating Rita* is frequently prescribed for examinations and I would not want to override the needs of students and their examiners (and indeed will do whatever I can to accommodate them) my main consideration is with the companies that act my plays and the audiences that watch them. And it is for this reason that I would like to make available this updated version of *Rita*. I haven't, in any way, radically over-hauled the text to the extent of changing the play itself. What I have done (and what proved to be enormously successful on the two occasions we produced it here in Liverpool last year) is to address those areas where there were very, very specific references to the time in which the play was originally written. Whilst I have not tried to reset the play in the 21st century, what I have done is cut and edit and rewrite in such a way that the play *can* be perceived as taking place in its own time (something that just wasn't possible when the text contained references to figures and institutions and attitudes firmly of the late 1970s / early 1980s). I'm convinced that, for any company, this version would be something of a bonus.

This revised text is set from the prompt copy of last year's Liverpool Playhouse production.

**Willy Russell**
**March 2003**

# ACT I

## Scene 1

*A book-lined tutorial room on the first floor of a Victorian-built university in the north of England*

*There is a large bay window with a desk placed in front of it. There is also another desk or table covered with various books and papers. On one wall there hangs a good and striking print of a nude, religious scene*

*Frank, who is in his early fifties, is standing holding an empty mug whilst pondering his shelves*

**Frank** Now where in the name of God... Eliot, Eliot...? (*He goes to one of the bookshelves and starts to remove books. He is puzzled*) Eliot? Emerson? E, E, E, Euripedes... (*With sudden enlightenment*) Ah! Eureka. D, D, D, D, Dickens! (*He replaces books and moves to another section of shelving jubilantly removing a couple of Dickensian tomes*) One can always rely on Dickens. (*He lifts out the books to reveal the bottle of scotch which has no more than about three or four fingers left in it; this he pours into his mug which he then raises in salute*) To my dear Charlie Dickens, genius and keeper of the scotch. (*He raises the mug to drink*)

*The phone rings, startling him slightly. Hurriedly he replaces the now empty bottle and the books before taking a gulp of the scotch and answering the phone*

Julia, Juliaa! ... Well yes, obviously I'm still here. ... Because I've got this Open University woman coming this evening, haven't I? ... Tch... Darling, I did tell you, of course I did. ... Well, then you shouldn't have prepared supper, should you? Because I said, darling, I distinctly recall saying that I would be late. ... Yes, yes, I probably *shall* go to the pub afterwards—I shall no doubt *need* to go to the pub afterwards if only to mercifully wash away some silly woman's attempts to get into the mind of Henry James or Thomas Hardy or whoever the hell it is we're supposed to study on this course... Christ, why did I take this on? ... Yes, darling, yes, I suppose I did take it on to pay for the drink. ... Oh, for God's sake, just leave it in the oven. ... Julia, if you're trying to induce feelings of guilt at the prospect of a charred dinner you'd have been better cooking something other than lamb and ratatouille. ... Because, my perfect poppet, I like my lamb cooked to the point of abuse and even a culinary ignoramus such as I knows that ratatouille is a dish that is impossible to overcook. ... Darling, you could incinerate ratatouille, radiate it, cook it in the ovens of hell, napalm the bloody stuff and still it wouldn't be overcooked! ... Determined to go to the pub? When did I need determination to get *me* into a pub...?

*There is a knock at the door*

Look, I'll have to go ... there's someone at the door. ... Yes, yes ... I ... all right, I promise ... just a couple of pints... (*sotto voce*) four...!

*Further, more insistent knocking at the door*

(*Calling in the direction of the door*) Come in! (*He continues into the phone*) Yes, I prom— all right ... yes, yes!

*More knocking from the door*

Come in! (*Into the phone*) Absolutely, darling, absolutely ... yes... bye-bye... (*He replaces the receiver*) Come in! COME IN!

*The door swings open, revealing Rita*

**Rita**  I *am* comin' in, aren't I? It's that stupid bleeding handle on the door. Y' wanna get it fixed!
**Frank**  Erm, yes. I erm... I er... I suppose I always meant to.
**Rita**  Well, that's no good, always meaning to, is it? Y' should get on with it. Because one of these days you'll be shouting "come in" and it'll go on forever and ever because the poor bastard on the other side of the door won't be able to come in. An' you won't be able to get out!
**Frank**  Now, you are?
**Rita**  What am I?
**Frank**  Pardon?
**Rita**  What?
**Frank**  (*prompting her now*) You are?
**Rita**  I'm a what?

*Frank busies himself with the papers on his desk. Rita is looking at the nude print. She becomes aware that Frank is watching her*

It's nice, isn't it? The picture, it's nice.
**Frank** Erm, yes, yes... I suppose it is, erm "nice".
**Rita** It's very erotic.
**Frank** Erm, well, I ... you know, I don't think I've actually really looked at it for the past ten years or so (*He switches the picture light on*) but ... yes, I suppose it is.
**Rita** There's no suppose about it—look at those tits.

*Frank again busies himself with the papers on his desk*

Is it supposed to be erotic? (*She's being quite genuine here—truly believing that those she regards as "educated people" can and do converse in such a way*) Like, when he painted it, do y' think he like, like meant it to be a turn on, y' know, sexually stimulating.
**Frank** (*fascinated as much as he is fazed by her*) Erm ... probably...
**Rita** I think he did, y' know. You don't paint pictures like that just so that people can admire the brush strokes, do y'?
**Frank** (*amused*) No. No, you're probably right.
**Rita** Because this was like the porn of its day, wasn't it? Y' know, before they had the videos; so this ... this is the sort of thing they would have perved over in those days, isn't it? But back then they had to pretend there was nothing erotic about it at all so that's why they made it religious, didn't they? Do you think it's erotic?
**Frank** I think it's very beautiful.
**Rita** I didn't ask you if it was beautiful.
**Frank** No. I know. But the term, "beautiful", covers the many feelings I have about the picture; including the feeling that yes, it is really rather erotic. (*He switches off the picture light*)
**Rita** D' y' get a lot like me?
**Frank** I beg your pardon?
**Rita** Do you get a lot of students like me.
**Frank** Not exactly, no.
**Rita** I was dead surprised when they accepted me. But I don't suppose they would have done if it had been a proper university, would they? It's different though, isn't it, the Open University? I suppose anyone can get in, can't they? D' y' think they must be desperate?
**Frank** I ... really couldn't say. I've not had much more experience of it than you have. In fact this is the first Open University work I've done.
**Rita** Oh, great! I end up with a beginner!
**Frank** No no, you misunderstand me; I work here at the university—I was just making the point that I haven't done this kind of extracurricular Open University work before.
**Rita** It was a joke!

**Frank** I am a bona fide lecturer but with...
**Rita** A joke!

*A beat*

**Frank** Oh, I'm sorry. Yes, of course, "a beginner", yes... (*He laughs now*)
**Rita** Quick? He's like lightnin'! So what y' doin' this for? D' y' need the money?
**Frank** Actually I do as a matter of fact.
**Rita** Oh.
**Frank** Erm ... would you like to sit down?
**Rita** No. Can I smoke?
**Frank** Tobacco?
**Rita** What?
**Frank** (*almost bashful*) A joke.
**Rita** (*not quite sure for a second*) Ogh. You mean was I gonna whip out the wacky-backy? I hate drugs. They just cover everything up. I hate them. (*She produces a packet of cigarettes and offers one to Frank*)
**Frank** (*hands aloft as if trying to physically ward off the temptation*) Ah ah... I'd love one.
**Rita** Well, have one!
**Frank** No, no really, I've given up.
**Rita** Everyone has. They're all afraid of gettin' cancer. But they're all cowards. You've got to challenge death an' disease. I read this great poem about fightin' death...
**Frank** Ah, Dylan Thomas.
**Rita** No, Roger McGough! It was all about this old man who runs away from hospital and goes out on the ale. He gets pissed and stands in the street shoutin' an' challengin' death to come out an' fight. It's brilliant.
**Frank** Mm. I don't think I'm familiar with the actual piece you mean.
**Rita** I'll bring y' the book; it's fantastic.
**Frank** Good, good. That's very kind of you.
**Rita** Mind you, you probably won't think it's any good at all.
**Frank** Why not?
**Rita** Because it's the sort of poetry you can understand.
**Frank** (*not quite sure*) Ah. Yes. I see. So you think it's important then, that poetry should be understood?
**Rita** (*shrugging*) Yeh. That's part of the reason I came here. Because there's loads that I don't understand.
**Frank** You mean poetry? A lot of poetry you don't understand?
**Rita** (*beginning to move around and scan the books on the shelves*) Yeh. All kinds of things.
**Frank** (*watching her for a second or two*) Look, can I offer you a drink?
**Rita** What of?

**Frank** Scotch?

**Rita** You should be careful with that stuff; it kills your brain cells, y' know.

**Frank** But you'll have one?

**Rita** (*going to the bookcase*) Yeh. All right. It'll probably have a job even finding my brain...

**Frank** (*scratching his head as he ponders the bookshelves, thinking out loud*) Now now now ... thinks, thinks ... F, F, F, Faulkner, Fielding ... ah, Forster... Forster! (*As he pulls away a couple of volumes of Forster, leaving them on the table desk, he reaches in and takes out another bottle of scotch which he then takes across to the small table*)

*Rita is silently gobsmacked for a second*

**Rita** My aunty's got a drinks cabinet like that!

**Frank** Water?

**Rita** No, I'll have the whisky. (*She picks up one of the Forster volumes*) What's this like?

**Frank** (*bringing the drinks across and looking at the book*) Howards End?

**Rita** Yeh. Sounds filthy, doesn't it? E.M. Foster.

**Frank** Forster!

**Rita** Forced her to do what?

**Frank** (*watching her for a second before breaking into real and appreciative laughter*) Forster, E.M. Forster; and it's doubtful that he would have forced "her" to do anything. Forster was a committed homosexual.

**Rita** Was he? Oh? So is that what his book's about, being gay?

**Frank** No, not at all. Actually it's about—but look, here... (*He hands her the book*) Borrow it. Read it for yourself.

**Rita** OK. Thanks. I'll look after it. If I pack the course in I'll post it back to y'.

**Frank** Pack it in? You've not even started yet. Why should you pack it in?

**Rita** I don't know. I just might. Might decide it was a stupid idea.

**Frank** If you're already contemplating the possibility of "packing it in", then why did you enrol in the first place?

**Rita** Because I want to know.

**Frank** *What*? What do you want to know?

**Rita** Everything.

**Frank** Everything? That's rather a lot, isn't it? Where were you thinking of beginning?

**Rita** Well... I'm a student now, aren't I? I'll have exams to do, won't I?

**Frank** Well, yes, eventually.

**Rita** So I'll have to learn about it all, won't I? It's like, y' sit there, don't y'—watchin' something like the ballet or the opera on the telly—an' y' just, y' know, call it rubbish because that's what it looks like, because y' don't understand—y' don't know how to see it—so y' just switch over or switch off an' say, "that's fuckin' rubbish".

**Frank** You do?

**Rita** Yeh. But I don't want to. Because I want to be able to see it. An' understand. Do you mind me swearin'?

**Frank** No, not at all.

**Rita** Do you swear?

**Frank** When I need to, yes, of course. I've never subscribed to the idea that there's such a thing as bad language—only bad *use* of language.

**Rita** See, the properly educated, they know it's only words, don't they? It's only the masses who don't understand. But that's because they're ignorant; it's not their fault, I know that, but sometimes they drive me mental. I do it to shock them sometimes; y' know if I'm in the hairdressers—that's where I work—I'll say somethin' like "I'm as fucked as a fanny on a Friday night!" and some of the customers, they'll have a right gob on them just 'cos I come out with something like that.

**Frank** Yes, but in the circumstances that's hardly...

**Rita** But it doesn't cause any kind of fuss with educated people though, does it? Because they know it's only words and they don't worry. But these stuck-up ones I meet, they think they're royalty just because they don't swear. An' anyway, I wouldn't mind but it's the aristocracy who swear more than anyone, isn't it, they're effing and blinding all day long; with them it's all, "I say, the grouse is particularly fucking lovely today although I'm afraid the spuds are a bit bollocks, don't you think?" (*She sighs*) But y' can't tell them that round our way. It's not their fault; they can't help it. But sometimes I hate them. (*Beat*) God ... what's it like to be free?

**Frank** Ah, now there's a question. Another drink?

**Rita** (*shaking her head*) Know if I'd got some other tutor I wouldn't have stayed.

**Frank** (*pouring himself another*) What do you mean, another tutor?

**Rita** Y' know, someone who objected to swearin'.

**Frank** How did you know that I wouldn't object?

**Rita** I didn't. I was just testin' y'.

**Frank** Yes! You're doing rather a lot of that, aren't you?

**Rita** I can't help it. That's what I do—y' know when I'm nervous.

**Frank** And how am I doing so far?

**Rita** (*with a noncommittal shrug; crossing to the window*) I love this room ... this window. Do you like it?

**Frank** What, the window?

**Rita** Yeh.

**Frank** It's not really something I consider, apart from those occasions when I feel an overwhelming urge to throw something through it.

**Rita** Like what?

**Frank** Oh, a student usually!

**Rita** (*amused*) You're bleedin' mad you, aren't y'?

**Frank** Quite possibly.

*Beat*

**Rita** Aren't you supposed to be interviewin' me?
**Frank** Do I need to?
**Rita** I know! I talk too much, don't I? I don't when I'm at home; I hardly ever talk at all when I'm there. But I don't often get the chance to talk to someone like you. Just tell me to shut up if I go on too much.
**Frank** I wouldn't dream of telling you to "shut up".
**Rita** What does "assonance" mean?
**Frank** (*laughing and spluttering his drink*) What the...
**Rita** Don't laugh at me.
**Frank** (*hearing the tone and knowing he's touched a nerve; quickly recovering*) No. No. Erm... I didn't mean... "Assonance". Well, it's, erm, it's a form of rhyme in which the corresponding vowels have the same sound but not the consonants that precede or follow the vowels. Now this can be slightly confusing because assonance can also be the use of identical consonants but with different vowels: erm, "killed/cold"... "draught/drift", "pin/pan", "gloom/gleam", "drink/drank"...
**Rita** (*involuntarily*) "Wink/Wank". (*She clasps a hand to her offending mouth*)
**Frank** (*delighted she's grasped it*) Yes, yes... that's right, that's right. Look, do you know Yeats?
**Rita** The wine lodge?
**Frank** (*taking down a book from his shelves*) The poet! W.B. Yeats, Irish poet. Look, you see, here... (*He shows her the relevant poem*) "The Wild Swans at Coole" and here, you see, see how he's using really subtle assonance, rhyming the word "swan" with the word "stone".
**Rita** So ... so "assonance" means gettin' the rhyme wrong?
**Frank** (*laughing in appreciation*) Well, yes ... yes, in a way, yes it does, it bloody well does, it means, "getting the rhyme wrong", but deliberately, purposefully in order to achieve a certain lyrical, almost musical effect.
**Rita** Oh. (*She sighs*) There's loads I don't know.
**Frank** Well, erm... It's Mrs White, is it?

*She nods*

But would you mind if I called you by your name, your first name?
**Rita** No.
**Frank** So what is it?
**Rita** My name? Oh, Rita.
**Frank** (*surprised; moving towards his desk*) Rita?

**Rita** Yeh.

**Frank** (*alluding to the papers on his desk*) But it says here Mrs "S" White.

**Rita** Oh that! Yeh, that's just "S" for "Susan". That's my real name. I've changed it to Rita though. I'm not a Susan anymore. I've called myself Rita—y' know, after Rita Mae Brown.

**Frank** (*blankly*) Who?

**Rita** Y' know, Rita Mae Brown—*Rubyfruit Jungle.* (*With serious reverence*) Rita Mae Brown, she wrote *Rubyfruit Jungle.*

**Frank** Ah.

**Rita** Have you not read it? It's fantastic. D' y' want me to lend it to y'?

**Frank** Erm, well, perhaps one day I might, erm...

*But it's too late because she is already pulling her well thumbed copy from her bag and showing it to him*

**Rita** And that's who I named myself after. 'Cos I just love that book. Do you wanna lend it?

**Frank** Oh ... um ... well ah...

*It's no good trying to avoid it. She presses it upon him*

**Rita** So what about you—what are you called?

**Frank** Frank.

**Rita** Oh, and were you named after someone?

**Frank** Well, not as far as I'm aware.

**Rita** Maybe your parents named you after the quality; y' know, "Frank", "frankness"—Elliot's brother——

**Frank** What?

**Rita** Y' know—Frank Ness. Elliot's brother. Elliot Ness.

**Frank** Oh! Elliot Ness. When you said Eliot I assumed you were referring to Tom—T.S. Eliot.

**Rita** T.S. Eliot? Have you read his stuff?

**Frank** Indeed I have, every last syllable.

**Rita** (*impressed*) Honest? I couldn't even get to the end of just one poem; I tried to read this thing called *J. Arthur Prufrock* but I couldn't make any bleeding sense of it at all. I just gave up.

*A beat*

I've not half got a lot to learn, haven't I?

**Frank** Did I hear you say you were a ladies' hairdresser?

**Rita** Yeh.

**Frank** Are you good at it?

**Rita** (*shrugging*) I am when I wanna be. Most of the time I don't wanna be, though. They get on my nerves.

**Frank** Who?

**Rita** The women, the customers. They never tell y' things that matter. Like, doin' a perm; well y' can't use a strong perm lotion on a head if it's been bleached with certain sorts of, y' know, cheap bleach. Because it makes all the hair break off, y' see. But at least once a month I'll get a customer comin' in for a perm an' she'll swear blind that she's had no bleaching done; but I can tell! I can see it. But she swears to God; so y' go ahead an' do the perm and she comes out the drier with half an inch of stubble.

**Frank** And are you able to do anything about that?

**Rita** Yeh. Flog her a wig!

**Frank** Good God!

**Rita** The pensioners are the worst—they're dead vain, y' know—it doesn't matter how old they are; so they'll never crack on if they're wearin' somethin' like a hearin' aid. So y' get your scissors an' start trimmin' away, next thing is, snip! Another granny gone deaf for a fortnight.

**Frank** You sound like something of a liability.

**Rita** I am. But they expect too much. They walk into the hairdressers and expect to walk out an hour later as a different person. I tell them, I'm just a hairdresser, not a plastic surgeon. See, most of them, that's why they come the hairdressers—because they want to be changed. But if you wanna change y' have to do it from the inside, don't y'? Know like I'm doin' ... tryin' to do. Do you think I will? Think I'll be able to do it.

**Frank** Well, that really depends upon you, on how committed you are. Are you sure that you're absolutely serious about this?

**Rita** I'm dead serious. Look, I know I take the piss an' that but I'm dead serious really. I am. I just take the piss because I'm not, y' know, confident. But I want to be. I want to know.

**Frank** Everything!

*She nods. He looks at her*

**Rita** What y' lookin' at me like that for?

**Frank** Because I think you're really rather marvellous.

**Rita** For God's sake! Now who's taking the piss?

**Frank** Don't you recognize a compliment?

**Rita** Oh, sod off!

**Frank** It's so long since I paid a compliment to anyone, I barely recognize it myself. (*He forces himself to change gear*) So! Come on; what I want to know is *why*—what is it that's suddenly led you to doing this?

**Rita** What, coming' here?

**Frank** Yes.

**Rita** Oh, it's not sudden. I've been realizin' for ages that I was ... slightly out of step. I'm twenty-six. I should have had a baby by now; everyone expects it—I'm sure my husband thinks I'm infertile. He's always goin' on about havin' babies. We've been tryin' for two years now; but I'm still on the pill! See, I don't want a baby yet. I wanna find myself first, discover myself. Do you understand that?

*He nods*

Yeh. They wouldn't round our way. I've tried to explain it to my husband but between you an' me I think he's just thick! No, not *thick*; blind, that's what he is. He can't see, because he doesn't *want* to see. If I try an' do anything different he get's a gob on him; even if I'm just reading or watchin' somethin' different on the telly he gets really narked. I just used to tell him to piss off but then I realized it was no good just doin' that an' what I should do is try an' explain to him. An' I tried; I tried explainin' to him how I wanted a better way of livin' my life. For once he listened. An' I even believed he understood because he said he felt the same as me—but all he meant was he was fed up livin' on our estate so we should start saving and try and move out to somewhere like Formby. Formby! Jesus, even if it was a new house I wanted I wouldn't move out to Formby. I hate that hole. Don't you?
**Frank** Mm.
**Rita** Whereabouts do you live?
**Frank** Oh, erm, up towards Southport.

*She realizes and cringes*

Can I offer you another drink?

*She shakes her head*

You don't mind if I do?
**Rita** It's your brain cells.
**Frank** All dead long ago, I'm afraid.

*But now any mirth/playfulness has evaporated from him. He drinks with a kind of grimness that has only previously been hinted at*

**Rita** When d' you actually, y' know, start teaching me?
**Frank** What can I possibly teach you?
**Rita** Everythin'.
**Frank** Everything.

*A beat*

I'll make a bargain with you, yes? I'll teach you everything I know ... but
if I do that then you must promise never to come back here ... because
there's nothing here for you! You see I never... I didn't want to teach this
course in the first place; allowed myself to be talked into it. But I knew it
was wrong and seeing you only confirms my suspicion. My dear, it's not
your fault, just the luck of the draw that you got assigned to me; but get me
you did. And the thing is, between you me and the walls, I'm really rather
an appalling teacher. Most of the time that doesn't really matter—
appalling teaching is quite in order when most of my students are
themselves fairly appalling. And the others manage to get by despite me.
But you, young woman, you are quite, quite different, you are seeking a
very great deal indeed; and I'm afraid I cannot provide it. Everything I
know—and you must listen to this—is that I know absolutely nothing.
(*Beat*) Added to which I don't like the hours of this Open University
malarkey, intolerably bloody unsocial—when the sun's gone over the
yardarm, my dear, I really should be in the pub! I can be really a rather good
teacher when I'm in the pub. Four pints of weak Guinness and I can be as
witty as Wilde, as pithy as Swift, as illuminating as ... well! I'm sorry.
There are other tutors—I'll make all the necessary arrangements and no
doubt the college will be in touch. (*He stands* DR *against the desk*)

*Rita slowly turns, collects her things and goes to the door. She goes out,
closing the door behind her. Suddenly though, the inner door handle is
being furiously turned as Rita tries to get back in. However, it being that
door it won't open again. We hear frantic and repeated knocking*

**Rita** (*off*) Let me in ... open this door ... let me back in ... open the door.
**Frank** (*calling*) Go away!
**Rita** (*off*) Wait a minute ... open this door ... listen...
**Frank** Leave me alone. There are other tutors, I've told you I——
**Rita** (*off*) *You're* my tutor! I don't want another tutor...
**Frank** For God's sake, woman! I've told you...
**Rita** (*off*) *You* are my tutor!
**Frank** I've told you, I don't *want* to teach you. Why come to me?

*And the door finally gives. Rita enters*

**Rita** Because you're a crazy mad piss artist who wants to throw his students
through the window. An' I *like* you. Don't you recognize a compliment?
And when I come back next week I'm gonna bring my scissors an' give
you a haircut.
**Frank** You are not coming back next week.

**Rita** I am! An' you're gettin' your hair cut.
**Frank** Oh, I don't think so.
**Rita** I suppose you wanna walk 'round like that, do y'?
**Frank** Like what?
**Rita** (*turning back just before she exits*) Like a geriatric hippy!

*Rita exits*

*Black-out*

SCENE 2

*The desk light is on*

*Frank is standing by the window, looking out. He glances at his watch and then peers out of the window again. He goes across to the bookcase, removes a few volumes and stares in at the bottle of scotch. For a moment he is tempted. But he resists and replaces the books. Walking away from the bookcase he goes to the window and looks out again. He glances at his watch once more. And then, changing his mind again:*

**Frank** Oh, sod it!

*He heads for the bookcase, pulling out books as he looks for the bottle. Only, as he does so he becomes aware of a noise. He turns and realizes that the door handle is being turned. Quickly replacing the books he moves towards the door, hesitating and then suddenly pulling it open to reveal Rita, oil can in hand. Frank switches on the light at the door*

**Rita** I was just oiling' it for y'. Well, I knew you'd never get around to it. (*Handing him the can as she brushes past him and enters the room*) Y' can have that.
**Frank** Oh! (*Dubiously*) Thank you.

*He watches as she wanders around the room*

**Rita** What y' lookin' at?
**Frank** Do you never just walk into a room and sit down?
**Rita** No. Not when it's a room like this. I love it.

*A beat*

How d' y' make a room like this?

**Frank** I don't *do* anything.
**Rita** Ah! That's the secret.
**Frank** There is no secret. I just moved in. And the rest just sort of ...
   happened.
**Rita** Yeh, that's 'cos you've got taste.

*A beat*

   I'm gonna have a room like this one day; there's nothin' phoney about it;
   everything's in it's right place. It's like wherever you've put something
   down ... it's grown to fit there.
**Frank** You mean it's a mess!
**Rita** Well, yeh. But ... but it's like ... it's like it's a lovely mess.
**Frank** Well... I suppose that over the years it might have acquired a certain
   patina.
**Rita** Yeh. That's what I meant. That sounds like a line from a romantic film,
   doesn't it? "Over the years your face has acquired a certain patina."

*A beat*

   You haven't been drinkin', have y'?
**Frank** Erm ... well, since you ask, no ... as a matter of fact.
**Rita** Is that because of me? Because of what I said to y' last week?
**Frank** What? You think where so many others have failed, *you* have
   reformed me!
**Rita** (*moving to the window*) I don't wanna reform y'. You can do what you
   like. (*Deliberately changing gear*) I love that lawn. It looks the way I
   always imagined somewhere like Eton or Harrow or one of those public
   schools to look. When I was a kid I always wanted to go to a boarding
   school.
**Frank** God forbid! Whatever for?
**Rita** I always thought they sounded great, schools like that. Y' know with
   a tuck shop and a matron and jolly hockey sticks; and there was always a
   pair of kids called Jones Major an' Jones Minor. I always loved that.
**Frank** What sort of a school *did* you go to?
**Rita** Just normal; like all the other schools by us; borin', ripped-up books,
   glass everywhere, knives and fights an' sadists—an' that was just the staff
   room. No, they tried their best, I suppose, always tellin' us we stood much
   more of a chance if we studied and worked hard. But studyin' was just for
   the geeks an' the wimps, wasn't it? See, if I'd started takin' school seriously
   then I would have had to become different from my mates; an' that's not
   allowed.
**Frank** Not allowed by whom?

**Rita** By y' mates, y' family, by everyone. So y' never admit that school could be anythin' other than useless an' irrelevant. An' what you've really got to be into are things like music an' clothes and gettin' pissed an' coppin' off an' all that kind of stuff. Not that I didn't go along with it because I did. But at the same time, there was always somethin' tappin' away in my head, tryin' to tell me I might have got it all wrong. But I'd just put the music back on or buy another dress an' stop worryin'. Cos there's always something that can make y' forget. An' so y' keep on goin', tellin' y'self that life is great—there's always another club to go to, a new feller to be chasin', a laugh an' a joke with the girls. Till one day, you just stop an' own up to yourself. Y' say, "Is this it? Is this the absolute maximum that I can expect from this livin' lark?" An' that's the really big moment that is. Because that is when you've got to decide whether it's gonna be another change of dress or a change in yourself. And it's really tempting to go out an' get that other dress. Because that way it's easy; y' know that you won't be upsettin' anyone or hurtin' anyone—apart from y'self! An' sometimes it's easier to do that, to take the pain y'self instead of hurtin' those around y'; those who don't want you to change.

**Frank** But ... you ... did it... You managed to resist another new dress

**Rita** You mean y' can't tell? Would y' look at the state of this? I haven't bought myself a new dress for the past twelve months. An' I'm not gonna get one either; not till I pass my first exam. An' then I'll get a proper dress, the sort of dress you'd only see on a educated woman, on the sort of woman who knows the difference between Jane Austin and ... erm ... and Ethel Austen!

*A beat*

OK. Can we start?

**Frank** Good idea. Yes, yes. (*He locates a couple of sheets of A4 paper on his desk*) All right; now look, this piece you wrote for me on, what was it called...

**Rita** *Rubyfruit Jungle* by Rita Mae Brown.

**Frank** Yes, well, the thing is, erm, it was, how can I say it...

**Rita** Shite?

**Frank** No no ... the thing is, it was an appreciation and erm, a reasonably structured outline of the plot. But you've made no attempt to explore whatever themes there are or how character is portrayed and developed or what kind of narrative is being employed. In short, you haven't really brought any criticism to bear.

**Rita** But I don't *want* to criticise *Rubyfruit Jungle*! Because I think it's brilliant!

**Frank** No no, I'm not talking about criticising, being critical in a censorious way; I'm talking about analytical criticism.

**Rita** What's the difference?
**Frank** Well, as far as possible you should approach criticism as being purely
objective. You see, you might consider ... erm ... what's it called...
**Rita** *Rubyfruit Jungle.*
**Frank** Yes, now you might consider ... *Rubyfruit Jungle*...
**Rita** By Rita Mae Brown.
**Frank** ...by Rita Mae Brown ... to be, what did you say, brilliant! But Rita,
that is *not* criticism; it is mere opinion. You see, it's subjective. And in
criticism there is no place for the subjective, for the sentimental, for the
partial or partisan. Literary criticism should be detached and thoroughly
supported by reference to established literary critique. Now bearing all of
that in mind I'd like you to give me a considered response to your reading
of *Howards End.*
**Rita** What, now?
**Frank** Yes. You have read it?
**Rita** Yeh! I've read it.
**Frank** So? (*Prompting*) *Howards End*?
**Rita** (*adopting suitable posture*) *Howards End* by Mr E.M. Forster is one
really crap book!
**Frank** What!
**Rita** In fact it's even crappier than crap!
**Frank** Oh really? And who the hell are you citing in support of that particular
thesis, F.R. Leavis?
**Rita** No! Me!
**Frank** What have I just said? *Me* is subjective!
**Rita** Well, it's what I think!
**Frank** You think one of the most considered novels of the twentieth century
is, "crap"! Well, perhaps you'll do me the courtesy of explaining *why* you
think it's, quote, "crap", unquote.
**Rita** Yeh, all right, yeh! I will tell y'! It's crap because the feller who wrote
it was a louse. Because halfway through that book I could hardly go on
readin' because he, Mr bleedin' E.M. Forster says, quote—"we are not
concerned with the poor"—unquote! That's why it's crap. That's why I
could barely keep on readin' it, that's why!
**Frank** (*astounded*) Because he said, "we are not concerned with the poor"?
**Rita** Yeh! That's right!
**Frank** But he wasn't writing about the poor.
**Rita** When he wrote that book the conditions of the poor in this country were
appalling an' he's sayin' he couldn't care less, Mr E.M. soddin' Foster.
**Frank** Forster!
**Rita** I don't really care what he was called—sittin' up there in his ivory tower
an' sayin' he couldn't care less.

*Frank begins to laugh*

Don't laugh at me!

**Frank** But this is madness! You cannot interpret E.M. Forster from a Marxist perspective.

**Rita** Why not?

**Frank** Look, before discussing any of this I said no subjectivity, no sentimentality.

**Rita** I wasn't being sentimental.

**Frank** Of course you were! You wanted Forster to concern himself with the poor. Literature can ignore the poor.

**Rita** Well, I think that's immoral.

**Frank** Amoral! (*Beat*) Have you any idea what kind of a mark you'd get if you approached Forster in this way during an examination?

**Rita** No! An' I don't care!

**Frank** Well, in that case we're going to have to *make* you care, aren't we? Because if I'm going to teach you and you're going to learn then I'm afraid you'll...

**Rita** All right! All right! But I hated that book. Can't we do somethin' else? Can't we do a book that I like?

**Frank** But books you *like* and books that will form the basis of your examination are extremely unlikely to be one and the same. The examiners, God help them, may never have heard of... *Rubyfruit Jungle* ... or Rita Mae Brown. And that is why you are going to have learn how to discipline that mind of yours, learn how to focus and concentrate and...

**Rita** Are you married?

**Frank** Oh, for God's sake!

**Rita** Are y' though? What's y' wife called?

**Frank** Is my wife of the remotest relevance here?

**Rita** Well, you should know that—you married her.

**Frank** All right! No, she's not relevant. We parted a long long time ago. OK?

**Rita** I'm sorry.

**Frank** Sorry for what?

**Rita** For asking. For bein' nosey.

**Frank** OK. But look, the thing about Forster and a book like *Howards End* is that...

**Rita** Why did you split up?

**Frank** (*after a beat*) Perhaps you'd like to take notes, mm? Then when you have to answer a question on Forster, you can treat the examiners to a dissertation on Frank's marriage!

**Rita** Oh, go 'way! It's only 'cos I'm interested.

**Frank** (*after a beat*) We split up, Rita, because of poetry.

**Rita** Go 'way.

**Frank** One day ... my then wife pointed out to me that for the preceding fifteen years my output as a poet had dealt exclusively with that brief period in which we had ... *discovered* each other.

**Rita** Are you a poet?

**Frank** *Was*—an extremely minor one—and so, to give me something fresh to fire the muse, she left me. A very selfless and noble woman, my ex-wife—she sacrificed her marriage for the sake of literature.

**Rita** An' what happened?

**Frank** Oh, it did the trick. My loss was literature's great gain.

**Rita** You started writing a whole load of good new stuff?

**Frank** No, I stopped writing altogether.

**Rita** (*after a beat*) Are you takin' the piss?

**Frank** No.

**Rita** People don't split up because of things like that, because of poetry an' literature...

**Frank** No?

**Rita** Did you never write any famous poems?

**Frank** (*laughing*) No. I published a couple of small collections. Sold a few here and there.

**Rita** Can y' still get them? I'll buy one of your books.

**Frank** I'm afraid they're all long out of print. And anyway I don't think it's the kind of stuff that you would have enjoyed.

**Rita** Why?

**Frank** Because, Rita, it's the sort of poetry that you *can't* understand! Unless, that is, you happen to have a detailed knowledge of literary allusion.

**Rita** So d' you live on your own now?

**Frank** No! I live with someone; an ex-student, she's now a tutor here. She's very caring, very tolerant, admires me enormously and spends a good deal of time with her head in the oven.

**Rita** Tryin' to kill herself.

**Frank** No, she just likes to watch the ratatouille cook or, as Julia's recently renamed it, "the stopout's stew".

**Rita** Is that you? Who stops out?

**Frank** Occasionally.

**Rita** For how long?

**Frank** (*slightly coy*) Two ... three days ... only now and then...

**Rita** Why?

**Frank** Now come on, look, that's enough of that; let's...

**Rita** If you were mine an' y' stopped out for days, y' wouldn't get back in!

**Frank** Ah, but Rita, if I was *yours* would I even consider stopping out for days?

**Rita** Don't you like her, Julia?

**Frank** I like her enormously. It's myself that I'm not too fond of.

**Rita** But you're great.

**Frank** A vote of confidence—thank you. Only, I'm afraid, Rita, that eventually you'll find there's less to me than meets the eye.

**Rita** See—you can say dead clever things like that. I wish I could just talk like that, it's brilliant.

**Frank** Yes, all right. Now, come on, *Howards End...*

**Rita** Oh hey! Leave that. I like just talkin' to y', it's great. That's what they do wrong in schools—they get y' goin' and then y' all havin' a great time talkin' about somethin' that's dead interestin' but the next thing is they wanna turn it into a lesson. Like we was out with this teacher once, y' know outside school on some project an' I'm right at the back with these other kids an' we saw this fantastic lookin' bird; it was all plumed an' coloured and dead out of place around our way. So I was just about to shout out an' tell Miss about it but this kid next to me said, "Keep y' mouth shut or she'll make us write a bleedin' essay on it!"

**Frank** (*ruefully*) Yes! It's what we do, Rita; we pluck birds from the sky and nail them down to learn how they fly.

**Rita** You'd think there was something wrong with education to hear you talk.

**Frank** Yes and perhaps there is.

**Rita** So why are y' givin' me an education?

**Frank** Because it's what *you* wanted. If it was up to me, what I'd like to do is take you by the hand and run out of this room forever.

**Rita** Oh, be serious!

**Frank** I am, Rita. I am! Right now there are a thousand things I'd rather do than teach—most of them with you, young woman.

**Rita** Oh, go way! You just like sayin' things like that!

**Frank** Do I?

**Rita** Y' know y' do.

**Frank** Oh Rita! Why didn't you walk in here twenty years ago?

**Rita** Because I don't think they would have accepted me at the age of six.

**Frank** You know what I mean.

**Rita** I know. But it's not twenty years ago, Frank. It's now—you're there an' I'm here.

**Frank** Yes and you're here for an education. Now come on! Forster.

**Rita** Oh, forget him!

**Frank** Now you listen to me! You want to learn, you want me to teach you. Well, that, I'm afraid, means a lot of work, for you as well as me. You've barely had a basic schooling, you've never even sat a formal examination let alone passed one. Possessing a hungry mind is not in itself a guarantee of any kind of success.

**Rita** All right, but I just don't like Howards bleedin' End.

**Frank** (*suddenly sharp*) Then go back to what you *do* like and stop wasting my time. You go off and buy yourself a new dress and I'll go to the pub! (*He switches off the desk light*)

*A beat*

**Rita** Is that you puttin' your foot down?
**Frank** Yes!
**Rita** Y' dead impressive when you're angry.
**Frank** Forster!
**Rita** (*picking up pen and essay papers*) All right, all right—Forster, Forster fuckin' Forster; "Does the repeated use of the phrase 'only connect' suggest that in reality E.M. Forster was a frustrated electrician?"

*Black-out*

## SCENE 3

*Frank is working at his desk, absorbed in re-reading Rita's essay as Rita herself rushes in, slightly out of breath, hurriedly removing her coat and quickly trying to get herself organised*

**Rita** Am I late? I'm sorry I'm late... I bleedin' hate it when that happens; I thought I'd easily be out of the shop by five tonight. I didn't have anyone booked in after four o'clock so I thought I'd easy get away by five, no worry. But bloody half past four one of my regulars showed up; could I do her a quick wash an' blow dry because she'd met this feller who's got a Chinese chippie in Childwall. *He's* not Chinese so it's not really a Chinese chippie—it's sort of ... must be fusion, I suppose. Well, he phoned her up out the blue this afternoon 'cos he's just copped a couple of tickets for an exhibition of state-of-the-art refrigeration units an' walk-in freezers. She said she doesn't even fancy him really. But she's always wanted a walk-in freezer herself...

*Rita finally becomes aware of Frank, staring at her as if she's something from another planet*

Oh God, I'm sorry, sorry; it's bein' in that shop everyday—I think it must be catching; that's what I have to listen to, all day every day. Anyway, I'm sorry I'm late. I hate bein' late when I'm comin' here.
**Frank** Let's forget about that. I want to talk about this that you sent me.
**Rita** (*knowing*) Oh, that!
**Frank** Yes! In response to the question, "Suggest how you might resolve the staging difficulties inherent in a production of Ibsen's *Peer Gynt*", you have written, quote, "Do it on the radio", unquote.
**Rita** Precisely!
**Frank** Precisely what?
**Rita** Precisely do it on the radio.

**Frank** And that is the entire essay?
**Rita** (*squirming*) Well ... we were ... we were just dead busy in the shop this week.
**Frank** You write your essays at work.

*She nods*

Why?
**Rita** Denny gets really pissed off if I work at home. He doesn't like me doin' this course. I can't be bothered arguin' with him.
**Frank** But you can't produce work that's as thin as this.
**Rita** Is it wrong?
**Frank** It's not a question of whether it's *wrong*. It's the fact of...
**Rita** See, I know it's on the short side ... but, but I thought it was the right answer.
**Frank** Well, it's the basis for an argument, Rita, but *one line* is hardly an essay.
**Rita** I know but I just didn't have much time this week so I sort ... sort of ... *encapsulated* all my ideas in one line.
**Frank** But it's not good enough.
**Rita** Why not?
**Frank** It just isn't.
**Rita** But that's bleedin' stupid because you say, don't y', that ... one line ... of exquisite poetry says ... infinitely more than a thousand pages of second rate prose.
**Frank** Yes. But you're not writing poetry! You are supposed to be writing an essay and what I'm trying to make you understand is that whoever was marking this would want more than "do it on the radio"! (*Changing gear*) Look, there's a way of answering examination questions that is ... expected. It's a sort of accepted ritual. It's a game, with rules. And you have to observe those rules. Poets can ignore those rules; poets can break every rule in the book; poets are not trying to pass examinations. But Rita, you are. And therefore you must observe the rules. When I was at university there was a student taking his final theology examination. He sat down in the hall, opened the exam paper, took out his pen and wrote, "God knows all the answers". Whereupon he handed in his paper, and left.
**Rita** (*impressed*) Did he?
**Frank** Yes, he did. And when it was time to collect his results he received a piece of paper on which were the words, "And God also gives out the marks!"
**Rita** Did he fail?
**Frank** Of *course* he failed! And rightly in my view because a clever answer is not necessarily the *best* answer.

**Rita** I wasn't tryin' to be clever; I was just run off me feet all this week so I never had time...

**Frank** All right, yes, yes, I know. But you have got some time now. And I want you to give it just a quarter of an hour or so adding some considered argument to this. "In attempting to resolve the staging difficulties in *Peer Gynt* I would present it on the radio because..." and then outline your reasons, supporting them wherever possible with quotes from accepted authorities. (*He switches the desk light on*) All right?

**Rita** Yeh. All right.

*Rita picks up her things and, helped by Frank, moves across to the second desk/table*

**Frank** Now you're sure you understand?

**Rita** D' you think I'm thick?

*As Rita settles herself at her desk, Frank returns to his own desk and busies himself reading and marking an essay. Rita finally gets down to work. But after a few moments she stops, deep in thought*

Y' know Peer Gynt? He was searchin' for the meaning of life, wasn't he?

**Frank** Put at its briefest, yes.

**Rita** Yeh.

*Beat*

I was doin' this woman's hair on Wednesday...

**Frank** Rita!

**Rita** I'm gonna do this, don't worry, I'll do it! But I just wanna tell y'; I was doin' her hair an' I was dead bored with what the others were talkin' about in the shop so I said to my customer, "Do you know about Peer Gynt?" She just thought it was a new kind of perm lotion! So I told her all about it, the play? An' y' know somethin', she was dead interested.

**Frank** (*disinterested*) Was she?

**Rita** She said to me, this woman, after I'd told her all about it, she said: "I wish *I* could go off searchin' for the meanin' of life". There's loads of them round by us who feel like that. Because there is no meaning!

*A beat as Rita ponders for a moment and Frank remains absorbed in his work*

Frank, y' know culture, know the word "culture", well, it doesn't just mean goin' to the opera an' the ballet and all that, does it?

**Frank** No.

**Rita** It means a way of livin', doesn't it? (*She pauses*) Well, we've got no culture.

**Frank** Who hasn't?

**Rita** Me; an' the people I come from—people I work with, live with, grew up with—us, we've got no culture.

**Frank** Of course you have.

**Rita** What? D' y' mean like that "working class culture" thing?

**Frank** Well ... yes.

**Rita** Yeh. I've read about that. I've never seen it though.

**Frank** Then look around you.

**Rita** I do. But I don't see any culture; I just see everyone pissed or stoned tryin' to find their way from one empty day to the next. There's more culture in a pot of yoghurt. Y' daren't say somethin' like that round our way though, because they're proud; an' they'll tell you we have got culture, doin' the pub quiz, goin' the club, singin' karaoke.

**Frank** But if they're content with that, if that's what people want then surely they've got the...

**Rita** But they *don't* want that! There is no contentment. Because there's no meanin' left. (*Beat*) Sometimes, when y' hear the old ones tellin' stories about the past, y' know, about the war or when they were all strugglin', fightin' for food and clothes and houses, their eyes light up while they're tellin' y' because there *was* some meanin' then. But what's ... what's stupid is that *now* ... now that most of them have got some kind of a house an' there is food an' money around, they're better off but, honest, they know they've got nothin' as well—because the meanin's all gone; so there's nothin' to believe in. It's like there's this sort of disease but no-one mentions it; everyone behaves as though it's normal, y' know, inevitable, that there's vandalism an' violence an' houses burnt out and wrecked by the people they were built for. But this disease, it just keeps on bein' hidden; because everyone's caught up in the "Got-To-Have-Game", all runnin' round like headless chickens chasin' the latest got-to-have tellies an' got-to-have cars, got-to-have haircuts an' got-to-have phones an' all the other got-to-have garbage that leaves y' wonderin' why you've still got nothin'— even when you've got it. (*Beat*) I suppose it's just like me, isn't it, y' know when I was buyin' dresses, keepin' the disease covered up all the time.

**Frank** (*after a beat*) Did you never consider taking a course in politics?

**Rita** Politics? Go 'way, I hate politics. I'm just tellin' y' about round our way. I wanna be on *this* course. You know what I learn from you about art an' literature, it feeds me, inside. I can get through the rest of the week if I know I've got comin' here to look forward to. (*Beat*) Denny tried to stop me comin' tonight. He tried to get me to go the pub with him an' his mates. He hates me comin' here. It's like druggies, isn't it? Addicts hate it when one of them tries to break away. It makes me stronger comin' here. That's what Denny's frightened of.

**Frank** "Only connect"!
**Rita** Oh, not faggie friggin' Forster again!
**Frank** "Only connect"—you see what you've been doing?
**Rita** Just tellin' y' about home.
**Frank** Yes, and connecting; your dresses/society at large/consumerism; drugs and addiction/you and your husband—connecting.
**Rita** Oh.
**Frank** You see?
**Rita** An' ... an' in that book ... no-one does connect.
**Frank** Yes! Irony.
**Rita** Is that it? Is that all it means?
**Frank** Not *all* of it but yes, that's the hub of it.
**Rita** Why didn't you just explain that to me right from the start?
**Frank** I could have done; but you'll have a much better understanding of something if you discover it in your own terms.
**Rita** Aren't you clever?
**Frank** Brilliant. Now! *Peer Gynt.*

*Rita returns to her desk and begins her work. Frank returns to his marking. We watch them, each absorbed in his/her work until Rita finishes writing, switches the desk lamp off and crosses to Frank's desk*

*(Eventually looking up)* What?
**Rita** I've done it.
**Frank** You've done it?

*Rita hands him the essay, from which he reads*

"In attempting to resolve the staging difficulties in a production of Ibsen's *Peer Gynt*, I would present it as a radio play because as Ibsen himself said, he wrote the play as a play for voices, never intending it to go on in a theatre. So if they had the radio in his day that's where he would have done it."

*He looks up at Rita who is beaming with unabashed pride and delight*

*Black-out*

SCENE 4

*There is an "atmosphere". Rita, still wearing outdoor coat/jacket, is standing, gazing out of the window, her back to Frank*

**Frank** What's wrong? You know this is getting to be a bit wearisome. When you come to this room you'll do anything except start work immediately. Couldn't you just come in prepared to work?

*Pause*

Where's your essay?
**Rita** I haven't got it.
**Frank** You haven't done it?
**Rita** I said I haven't *got* it.
**Frank** You've lost it?
**Rita** No.
**Frank** Don't tell me! Last night, whilst you were asleep a couple of errant Oxbridge dons broke into your premises and appropriated your essay for their own highly dubious ends.

*No reaction*

(*Gently*) Rita!

*She turns to face him*

**Rita** It's burnt.
**Frank** Burnt?
**Rita** So are all the Chekhov books you lent me. Denny found out I was still on the pill; it was my own fault, I'd left me prescription out. He burnt all me books.
**Frank** Oh Christ!
**Rita** I'm sorry. I'll buy y' some more.
**Frank** I wasn't referring to the books. Sod the books.
**Rita** Why can't he just let me get on with my learnin'? You'd think I was havin' a fuckin' affair the way he behaves.
**Frank** And aren't you?
**Rita** No! What time have I got for an affair? I'm busy enough findin' myself, let alone findin' someone else. I don't want anyone else. I've begun to find me—an' it's great, y' know, it is, Frank. It might sound selfish but all I want for the time bein' is what I'm findin' inside me. I certainly don't wanna be rushin' off with some feller, 'cos the first thing I'll have to do is forget about myself for the sake of him.
**Frank** Perhaps ... perhaps your husband thinks you're having an affair with me.
**Rita** Oh, go 'way. You're just me teacher. I've told him.
**Frank** You've told him about me? What?
**Rita** I've—tch—I've tried to explain to him how you give me room to breathe. You just, like feed me without expectin' anythin' in return.

**Frank** (*after a beat*) And what did he say to that?
**Rita** He didn't. I was out for a while. When I came back he'd burnt me books an' papers, most of them. I said to him y' soft get, even if I was havin' an affair there's no point burnin' me books, is there. I'm not havin' it off with Anton Chekhov! He said, "I wouldn't put it past you to shack up with a foreigner".
**Frank** What are you going to do?
**Rita** I'll order some new copies for y' an' I'll do the essay again.
**Frank** I mean about your husband.
**Rita** I've told him, I said, "There's no point cryin' over spilt milk, most of the books are gone, but if you touch my *Peer Gynt* I'll kill y'".
**Frank** Tch. Be serious.
**Rita** I was!
**Frank** Do you love him?
**Rita** I see him lookin' at me sometimes, an' I know what he's thinkin; he's wonderin' where the girl he married has gone to. He even brings me presents sometimes, hopin' that the presents'll make her come back. But she can't, because she's gone, an' I've taken her place.
**Frank** Do you want to abandon this course?
**Rita** No. No!
**Frank** When art and literature begin to take the place of life itself, perhaps it's time to...
**Rita** But it's *not* takin' the place of life, it's *providin'* me with life. He wants to take life away from me; he wants me to stop rockin' the coffin, that's all. Comin' here, doin' this, it's given me more life than I've had in years, an' he should be able to see that. Well, if he doesn't see that, if he doesn't want me when I'm alive, then I'm certainly not just gonna lie down an' die for him. I told him I'd only have a baby when I had a choice. But he doesn't understand. He thinks we've got choice because we can go into a pub that sells eight different kinds of lager. He thinks we've got choice already: choice between Everton an' Liverpool, choosin' which washin' powder, choosin' between one shitty school an' the next, between jobs for jokers or stayin' on the dole. He thinks we've *got* choice already because there's thirty-eight satellite channels to watch.
**Frank** Yes. Well, perhaps your husband——
**Rita** No! I don't come here to talk about him. Why was Chekhov a comic genius?
**Frank** Rita! Don't you think that for tonight we could give the class a miss?
**Rita** No, I want to know. I've got to do this. He can burn me books an' me papers but if it's all in my head then he can't touch it. It's like that with you, isn't it? You've got it all inside.
**Frank** Let's leave it for tonight. Let's go to the pub and drink pots of Guinness and talk.

26                                                        Educating Rita

**Rita** I've got to do this, Frank. I've got to. I want to talk about Chekhov.
**Frank** You don't think you should be talking about you and your husband?
**Rita** I don't *want* to.
**Frank** (*recognizing the determination*) All right, OK... (*He goes to the bookcase and lifts down books*) Chekhov. C for Chekhov. We'll talk about Chekhov and pretend *this* is the pub.
**Rita** (*seeing the bottles*) Why d' y' keep it stashed behind there?
**Frank** A little arrangement I have with my immediate employers. It's called "discretion". They didn't tell me to stop drinking, they told me to stop displaying the signs.
**Rita** Do you actually *like* drinking?
**Frank** I adore it. You see, Rita, the great thing about the booze is that one is never bored when drinking. Or boring for that matter; the booze has this marvellous capacity for making one believe that underneath all the talk one is actually *saying* something.
**Rita** (*after a beat*) Know when you were a poet, Frank, did you drink then?
**Frank** Some. Not as much as now.
**Rita** Why did you stop being a poet?
**Frank** That is a pub question.
**Rita** Well. I thought we were pretendin' this was the pub.
**Frank** In which we would discuss Chekhov!
**Rita** Well, he's second on the bill. You're on first. Go on, why did you stop?
**Frank** (*sighing*) I didn't *stop*, Rita, so much as realize I never was. I'd simply got it wrong. Instead of creating poetry I spent—oh—years trying to create literature.
**Rita** But ... but I thought that's what poets did.
**Frank** What?
**Rita** Y' know, create literature.
**Frank** No no no; poets should confine themselves to creating poetry; poets should do their damndest not to believe in literature.
**Rita** I don't understand that.
**Frank** You will, Rita; one day you will.
**Rita** Huh. Sometimes I wonder if I'll ever understand any of it. It's like startin' all over again, y' know with a different language. Like I read that Chekhov play an' I thought it was dead sad, it was tragic; people committin' suicide an' the Constantin kid's tryin' to produce his masterpiece while they're all laughin' at him? It is, it's tragic. But then I read the blurb about it an' everyone's goin' on about Chekov bein' this comic genius'.
**Frank** Yes, but they don't mean comedy like—erm—well, it's not jokes, gags; it's not ... stand-up comedy. Have you ever seen Chekhov in the theatre?
**Rita** No. Does he go?
**Frank** Have you ever been to the theatre?

**Rita**  No.
**Frank**  You should, you should go.
**Rita**  Hey! Why don't we go tonight?
**Frank**  Me go to the theatre? God, no, I detest the theatre.
**Rita**  Well, why the hell are y' sendin' me?
**Frank**  Because *you* want to know.
**Rita**  Well, you come with me.
**Frank**  Oh, certainly! And how would I explain that to Julia?
**Rita**  Just tell her y' comin' to the theatre with me.
**Frank**  "Julia, I shall not be in for dinner tonight as I am going to the theatre with ravishing Rita."
**Rita**  Oh, sod off.
**Frank**  I'm being quite serious.
**Rita**  Would she really be jealous?
**Frank**  If she knew I was at the theatre with an irresistible thing like you? Rita, it would be deaf and dumb breakfasts for a week.
**Rita**  Why?
**Frank**  Why not?
**Rita**  I dunno—I just thought...
**Frank**  Rita, as ludicrous as it may seem to you, even a woman who possesses an MA is not above common jealousy.
**Rita**  Well, what's she got to be jealous of me for? I'm not gonna try an' rape y' in the middle of *The Seagull*.
**Frank**  What a terrible pity. You just might have made theatre exciting for me again.
**Rita**  Come on, Frank. Come with me. Y' never tell the truth you, do y'?
**Frank**  What do y' mean?
**Rita**  You always ... *evade* it, don't y', with jokes an' that. Come on, come to the theatre with me. We'll have a laugh...
**Frank**  Will we?
**Rita**  Yeh. C'mon, we'll ring Julia. (*She picks up Frank's phone*)
**Frank**  What?
**Rita**  C'mon, what's your number?
**Frank**  (*taking the receiver from her and replacing it*) We will *not* ring Julia. Anyway, Julia's out tonight.
**Rita**  So what will you do, spend the entire night in the pub?
**Frank**  Yes.
**Rita**  Come with me, Frank, y'll have a better time than y' will in the pub.
**Frank**  Will I?
**Rita**  Course y' will.
**Frank**  (*considering*) What is it you want to see?
**Rita**  *The Importance of Bein'* ... what's-his-name.
**Frank**  *The Importance*? It's not on at the moment.

**Rita**  It is—I passed the church hall on the bus an' there was a poster...
**Frank**  An *amateur* production?
**Rita**  What?
**Frank**  Are you suggesting I miss a night in the pub to watch *The Importance of Being Earnest* played by a bunch of bloody amateurs in a church hall?
**Rita**  It doesn't matter who's doin' it! It's the same play, isn't it?
**Frank**  Well! I wouldn't be so sure of that, Rita...
**Rita**  Oh, come on—hurry up—I'm dead excited. I've never seen a live play before.

*During the following they prepare to leave the room—collecting bags, coats, switching off lamps*

**Frank**  And there's no guarantee you'll see a "live" play tonight.
**Rita**  Why? Just 'cos they're amateurs? Y've got to give them a chance, Frank. They have to learn somewhere. An' anyway, they might be good.
**Frank**  Yes...
**Rita**  Oh, you're an awful snob, aren't y'?
**Frank**  Am I? All right then—come on. (*He switches off the desk lamp*)
**Rita**  Have you seen it before?
**Frank**  Of course I have. (*He switches off the standard lamp*)
**Rita**  Well, don't you go tellin' me what happens, will y'? Don't go spoilin' it for me.

*They exit*

*Black-out*

SCENE 5

*It is lunchtime as Frank enters*

*He puts down his things, switches on the radio (Radio Four) from which we hear the weather forecast directly preceeding* The World At One. *Frank takes out his lunch and sits at his desk eating and reading a book, the cover of which we recognize as being* Rubyfruit Jungle

*Rita suddenly burts into the room, out of breath from running*

*Frank switches the radio off*

**Frank**  What are you doing here? It's Thursday, you...

**Rita** I know I shouldn't be here, it's me dinner hour, but listen, I've got to tell someone, have y' got a few minutes, can y' spare——

**Frank** My God, what is it?

**Rita** I had to come an' tell y', Frank, last night, I went to the theatre! A proper one, a professional theatre.

**Frank** For God's sake, you had me worried, I thought it was something serious.

**Rita** It was, it was Shakespeare, I thought it was gonna be dead borin' but it wasn't—it was brilliant. I'm gonna do an essay on it.

**Frank** Come on, which one was it?

**Rita**             "...Out, out, brief candle!
Life's but a walking shadow, a poor player
That struts and frets his hour upon the stage
And then is heard no more. It is a tale
Told by an idiot, full of sound and fury
Signifying nothing."

**Frank** Ah, *Romeo and Juliet*.

**Rita** Tch. Frank! Be serious. I learnt that today from the book. Look, I went out an' bought the book. Isn't it great? What I couldn't get over is how excitin' it was. Wasn't his wife a cow, eh? An' that fantastic bit where he meets Macduff an' he thinks he's all invincible. I was on the edge of me seat at that bit. I wanted to shout out an' tell Macbeth, warn him.

**Frank** You didn't, did you?

**Rita** Nah. Y' can't do that in a theatre, can y'? It was brilliant though. It was like a thriller.

**Frank** Well, you'll have to go and see more Shakespeare.

**Rita** I'm goin' to. *Macbeth*'s a tragedy, isn't it?

**Frank** Yes, it is.

**Rita** Right.

*Beat*

Well, I just—I just had to tell someone who'd understand.

**Frank** I'm honoured that you chose me.

**Rita** I better get back. I've left a customer in the shop. If I don't get a move on there'll be another tragedy.

**Frank** No. There won't be a tragedy.

**Rita** There will, y' know. I know this woman, she's dead fussy. If her lo' lights don't come out right there'll be blood an' guts everywhere.

**Frank** Which might be quite tragic—but it won't be a tragedy.

**Rita** What?

**Frank** Well—erm—look; the tragedy of the drama has nothing to do with the sort of tragic event you're talking about. Macbeth is flawed by his ambition—yes?

**Rita**  Yeh. Go on.

**Frank**  Erm—it's that flaw which forces him to take the inevitable steps towards his own doom. You see? Whereas, Rita, a woman's hair being ruined, or—or the sort of thing you read in the paper that's reported as being tragic, "Man Killed by Falling Tree", that is *not* a tragedy.

**Rita**  It is for the poor sod under the tree.

**Frank**  Yes, it's *tragic*, absolutely tragic. But it's not a *tragedy* in the way that *Macbeth* is a tragedy. You see, in dramatic terms, tragedy is something that is absolutely inevitable, pre-ordained almost. Now, look, even without ever having even heard the story of *Macbeth* you wanted to shout out, to warn him and prevent him going on, didn't you? But you wouldn't have been able to stop him, would you?

**Rita**  No.

**Frank**  And why is that?

**Rita**  'Cos they would have thrown me out of the theatre.

**Frank**  No no no no, what I mean is that your warning would have been ignored. He's warned in the play, constantly warned. But he can't go back. He still treads the path to doom. But, you see, the poor old fellow under the tree hasn't arrived there by following any inevitable steps, has he?

**Rita**  No.

**Frank**  There's no particular flaw in his character that has dictated his end. If he'd been warned of the consequences of standing beneath that particular tree he wouldn't have done it, would he? Understand?

**Rita**  So ... so Macbeth brings it on himself?

**Frank**  Yes! You see, he goes blindly on and on and with every step he's spinning one more piece of thread which will eventually make up the network of his own tragedy. You see that?

**Rita**  I think so. I'm not used to thinkin' like this.

**Frank**  It's quite easy, Rita.

**Rita**  It is for you. I just thought it was a dead excitin' story. But the way you tell it you make me see all sorts of things in it. It's fun, tragedy, isn't it? (*She indicates the window and beyond*) All them out there. They know all about that sort of thing, don't they?

**Frank**  Look, what are you doing for lunch?

**Rita**  (*heading for the door*) Lunch? Christ—me customer. She only wanted lo' lites—she'll come out looking like she's got fuckin' laser lights! (*She turns back*) Ey, Frank, listen—I was thinkin' of goin' to the art gallery tomorrow. It's me half day off. D' y' wanna come with me?

**Frank**  All right. (*Beat*) And—look, what are you doing on Saturday?

**Rita**  I work.

**Frank**  Well, when you finish work?

**Rita**  Dunno.

**Frank**  I want you to come over to the house.

**Rita** Why?
**Frank** Julia's organized a few people to come round for dinner.
**Rita** An' y' want *me* to come?
**Frank** Yes.
**Rita** Why?
**Frank** Why do you think?
**Rita** I don't know.
**Frank** Because you might *enjoy* it.
**Rita** Oh.
**Frank** Will you come?
**Rita** If y' want.
**Frank** What do *you* want?
**Rita** All right, I'll come.
**Frank** Will you bring Denny?
**Rita** I don't know if he'll come.
**Frank** Well, ask him!
**Rita** All right.
**Frank** What's wrong?
**Rita** What shall I wear?

*Black-out*

SCENE 6

*Frank and Rita are sitting in their usual places*

**Frank** Now I don't mind; two empty seats at the dinner table means more of the vino for me. But Julia—Julia is the stage manager type. If we're having eight people to dinner she expects to see eight. She likes order—probably why she took me on—it gives her a lot of practice—and having to cope with six instead of eight was extremely hard on Julia. I'm not saying that *I* needed any sort of apology; you don't turn up, that's up to you, but...
**Rita** I did apologize.
**Frank** "Sorry couldn't come", scribbled on the back of your essay and thrust through the letter box? Rita, that's hardly an apology.
**Rita** What does the word "sorry" mean if it's not an apology? When I told Denny we were goin' to yours he went mad. We had a big fight about it.
**Frank** I'm sorry. I didn't realize. But look, couldn't you have explained. Couldn't you have said that was the reason?
**Rita** No. 'Cos that wasn't the reason. I told Denny if he wasn't gonna go I'd go on me own. An' I tried to. All day Saturday, all day in the shop I was thinkin' what to wear. Got home, tried on all kinds of dresses. Everythin'

looked bleedin' awful. An' all the time I'm trying to think of things I can
say, what I can talk about. An' I can't remember anythin'. It's all jumbled
up in me head. I can't remember if it's Wilde who's witty an' Shaw who
was Shavian or who the hell wrote *Howards End*.

**Frank** Ogh Christ!

**Rita** Then I got the wrong bus to your house. It took me ages to find it. Then
I walked up your drive, an' I saw y' all through the window, you were
sippin' drinks an' talkin' an' laughin'. An' I couldn't come in.

**Frank** Of course you could.

**Rita** I couldn't! I'd bought the wrong sort of wine. When I was in the off
licence I knew I was buyin' the wrong stuff. But I didn't know which was
the right wine.

**Frank** Rita, for Christ's sake; I wanted *you* to come along. You weren't
expected to dress up or buy wine.

**Rita** If you go out to dinner, don't you dress up? Don't you take wine?

**Frank** Yes, but...

**Rita** Well?

**Frank** Well what?

**Rita** Well, you wouldn't take sweet sparkling wine, would y'?

**Frank** Does it matter what I do? It wouldn't have mattered if you'd walked
in with a bottle of Spanish plonk.

**Rita** It *was* Spanish.

**Frank** Why couldn't you relax? It wasn't a fancy dress party. You could
have come as yourself. Don't you realize how people would have seen you
if you'd just—just breezed in? Mm? They would have seen someone
who's funny, delightful, charming...

**Rita** But I don't want to be charming and delightful; *funny*, what's *funny*?
I don't want to be *funny*. I wanna talk seriously with the rest of you, I don't
wanna spend the night takin' the piss, comin' on with the funnies because
that's the only way I can get into the conversation. I didn't want to come
to your house just to play the court jester.

**Frank** You weren't being asked to play that role. I just—just wanted you to
be yourself.

**Rita** But I don't want to be myself. Me? What's me? Some stupid woman
who gives us all a laugh because she thinks she can learn, because she
thinks that one day she'll be like the rest of them, talking seriously,
confidently, with knowledge, live a civilized life. Well, she can't be like
that really but bring her in because she's good for a laugh.

**Frank** (*erupting*) If you believe that that's why you were invited, to be
laughed at, then you can get out of here right now. You were invited
because I wished to have your company and if you can't believe that then
I suggest you stop visiting me and start visiting an analyst who can cope
with matters such as paranoia.

**Rita** I'm all right with you, here in this room; but when I saw those people you were with I couldn't come in. I would have seized up. Because I'm a freak. I can't talk to the people I live with any more. An' I can't talk to the likes of them on Saturday, or them out there, because I can't learn the language. I'm an alien. I went back to the pub where Denny was, an' me mother, an' our Sandra, an' her mates. I'd decided I wasn't comin' here again. I went into the pub an' they were singin', all of them singin' some song they'd learnt from the juke-box. An' I stood in that pub an' thought, just what in the name of Christ am I trying to do? Why don't I just pack it in, stay with them, an' join in with the singin'?

**Frank** And why don't you?

**Rita** You think I can, don't you? Just because you pass a pub doorway an' hear the singin' you think we're all OK, that we're all survivin', with the spirit intact. Well, I *did* join in with the singin', I didn't ask any questions, I just went along with it. But when I looked round, my mother had stopped singin', an' she was cryin'. Everyone just said she was pissed an' we should get her home. So we did, an' on the way I asked her why. I said, "Why are y' cryin', Mother?" She said, "Because—because we could sing better songs than those". Ten minutes later, Denny had her laughing and singing again, pretending she hadn't said it. But she had. And that's why I came back. And that's why I'm staying.

*Black-out*

SCENE 7

*Frank is absorbed in marking some papers*

*When Rita enters, she is carrying a large holdall*

**Frank** One second. (*He finishes marking, looks up and sees the holdall*) What's that?

**Rita** (*struggling to control herself throughout the following*) It's my bag. My things.

**Frank** Where are you going?

**Rita** My mother's.

**Frank** What's wrong? Rita.

**Rita** I got home from work, he'd packed my bag. He said either I stop comin' here an' come off the pill or I could get out altogether.

**Frank** Ogh ... fuck.

**Rita** It was an ultimatum. I explained to him. I didn't get angry or anythin', I just explained to him how I *had* to do this. But he said it's warped me. He said I'd betrayed him. I suppose I have.

**Frank** *How* have you betrayed anyone?
**Rita** I have. I know he's right. But I couldn't betray meself. He says there's a time for education. An' it's not when y' twenty-six an' married.
**Frank** Where are you going to stay?
**Rita** I phoned me mother; she said I could go there for a week. Then I'll get a flat. I'm sorry, it's just... (*Although still struggling fiercely to deny her tears she momentarily loses the battle*)
**Frank** Look, come on, sit down.

*Refusing to be comforted, Rita moves away to the window*

**Rita** It's all right—I'll be OK. Just ... just give me a minute. (*She turns back. Although the tears are now flowing she will not give in to them*) What was me *Macbeth* essay like?
**Frank** Oh, sod *Macbeth*.
**Rita** Why?
**Frank** Rita!
**Rita** No, come on, come on, I want y' to tell me what you thought about it.
**Frank** Rita, in the circumstances I really...
**Rita** It doesn't matter, it doesn't! In the circumstances I need to go on, to talk about it an' do it. What was it like? I told y' it was no good. Is it really useless?
**Frank** I—I really don't know what to say.
**Rita** Well, try an' think of somethin'. Go on, I don't mind if y' tell me it was rubbish. I don't want pity, Frank. Was it rubbish?
**Frank** No, no. Not rubbish. (*He picks up the papers he was marking earlier*) It's a totally honest, passionate account of your reaction to a play. It's an unashamedly emotional statement about a particular experience.
**Rita** Sentimental?
**Frank** No no. It's far too honest for that. It's almost—erm—moving. But in terms of what you're asking me to teach you of passing exams... Oh, God, you see, I don't...
**Rita** Say it, go on, say it!
**Frank** In those terms it's worthless. It shouldn't be, but it is; in its own terms it's—it's wonderful.
**Rita** It's worthless! You said. An' if it's worthless you've got to tell me because I want t' write essays like those on there. I want to know, an' pass exams like they do.
**Frank** But if you're going to write this sort of stuff you're going to have to change.
**Rita** All right. Tell me how to do it.
**Frank** But I don't know if I want to tell you, Rita, I don't know that I want to teach you. What you already have is valuable.

**Rita** Valuable? What's valuable? The only thing I value is here, comin' here once a week.

**Frank** But, don't you see, if you're going to write this sort of thing—to pass examinations, you're going to have to suppress ... perhaps even abandon your uniqueness. I'm going to have to change you.

**Rita** But don't you realize, I *want* to change! Listen, is this your way of tellin' me that I can't do it? That I'm no good?

**Frank** It's not that at——

**Rita** If that's what you're tryin' to tell me I'll go now——

**Frank** No no no. Of course you're good enough.

**Rita** See, I know it's difficult for y' with someone like me. But you've just gorra keep tellin' me an' then I'll start to take it in; y' see, with me you've got to be dead firm. You won't hurt me feelings, y' know. If I do somethin' that's crap, I don't want pity, you just tell me, that's crap. Here, it's crap. Right. So we dump that in the bin, an' we start again. (*She sits on the chair* RC)

*Black-out*

CURTAIN

# ACT II

## SCENE 1

*Frank is sitting at his desk typing. He pauses, takes a sip from the mug at his side, looks at his watch and then continues typing*

*Rita bursts through the door. She is dressed in "new", second-hand clothes*

**Rita** Frank! (*She twirls to show off her new clothes*)
**Frank** (*smiling*) And what is this vision, returning from the city? (*He gets up and moves towards Rita*) Welcome back.
**Rita** Frank, it was fantastic. (*She takes off her shawl and gives it to Frank*)

*He hangs it on the hook by the door. Rita goes to the desk*

(*Putting down her bag on the desk*) Honest, it was—ogh!
**Frank** What are you talking about, London or summer school?
**Rita** Both. A crowd of us stuck together all week. We had a great time: dead late every night, we stayed up talkin', we went all round London, got drunk, went to the theatres, bought all sorts of second-hand gear in the markets... Ogh, it was...
**Frank** So you won't have had time to do any actual work there?
**Rita** Work? We never stopped. Lashin' us with it they were; another essay, lash, do it again, lash.

*Frank moves towards the desk*

Another lecture, smack. It was dead good though. (*She goes and perches on the bookcase*)

*Frank sits in the swivel chair, facing her*

Y' know at first I was dead scared. I didn't know anyone. I was gonna come home. But the first afternoon I was standin' in the library, y' know, lookin' at the books, pretendin' I was dead clever. Anyway, this tutor come up to me, he looked at the book in me hand an' he said, "Ah, are you fond of Ferlinghetti?" It was right on the tip of me tongue to say, "Only when it's served with Parmesan cheese", but, Frank, I didn't. I held it back an' I heard meself sayin', "Actually, I'm not too familiar with the American poets". Frank, you woulda been dead proud of me. He started talkin' to me about the Beat poets—we sat around for ages—an' he wasn't even one of my official tutors, y' know. We had to go to this big hall for a lecture, there must have been two thousand of us in there. After he'd finished his lecture this professor asked if anyone had a question, an', Frank, I stood up! (*She stands*) Honest to God, I stood up, an' everyone's lookin' at me. I don't know what possessed me, I was gonna sit down again, but two thousand people had seen me stand up, so I did it, I asked him the question.

*There is a pause and Frank waits*

**Frank** Well?
**Rita** Well what?
**Frank** What was the question?
**Rita** Oh, I dunno, I forget now, 'cos after that I was askin' questions all week, y' couldn't keep me down. I think that first question was about Chekhov; 'cos y' know I'm dead familiar with Chekhov now.

*He smiles, Rita moves to the chair by the desk and sits. Frank swivels round to face her*

Hey, what was France like? Go on, tell us all about it.
**Frank** There isn't a lot to tell.
**Rita** Ah, go on, tell me about it; I've never been to France. Tell me what it was like.
**Frank** Well—it was rather hot... I've brought you back something. (*He hands her a duty-free pack of 200 Gauloise cigarettes*)
**Rita** I've packed it in. Did y' do much drinkin' over there?
**Frank** Ah—a little. (*He puts the cigarettes on the table*)
**Rita** Tch. Did y' write?
**Frank** A little.
**Rita** Will y' show it to me?
**Frank** Perhaps... One day, perhaps.
**Rita** So y' wrote a bit an y' drank a bit? Is that all?
**Frank** (*in a matter of fact way*) Julia left me.
**Rita** What?
**Frank** Yes. But not because of the obvious, oh no—it had nothing whatsoever to do with the ratatouille. It was actually caused by something called *oeufs en cocotte*.
**Rita** What?
**Frank** Eggs, my dear, eggs. Nature in her wisdom, cursed me with a dislike

for the egg, be it cocette, Florentine, Benedict or plain hard-boiled. Julia insisted that nature was wrong. I defended nature and Julia left.

**Rita** Because of eggs?

**Frank** Well—let's say that it began with eggs. (*He packs away the typewriter*) Anyway, that's most of what happened in France. But now the holiday's over, you're back, even Julia's back.

**Rita** Is she? Is she all right?

**Frank** (*putting the typewriter on the window desk and the sheets of paper in the top left drawer*) Perfect. I get the feeling we shall be together forever; or until she discovers *oeufs à la crécy*.

**Rita** *Oeufs à la crécy*? Does that mean eggs? Trish was goin' on about those; is that all it is, eggs?

**Frank** Trish?

**Rita** Trish, me flatmate, Trish. God, is it that long since I've seen y', Frank? She moved into the flat with me just before I went to summer school.

**Frank** Ah. Is she a good flatmate?

**Rita** She's great. Y' know she's dead classy. Y' know, like she's got taste, y' know, like you, Frank, she's just got it. Everything in the flat's dead unpretentious, just books an' plants everywhere. D' y' know somethin', Frank? I'm havin' the time of me life; I am, you know. I even feel—(*she moves to the window*)—I feel young, you know, like them down there.

**Frank** My dear, twenty-six is hardly old.

**Rita** I know that; but I mean, I feel young like them... I can be young. (*She goes to her bag*) Oh, listen. (*She puts the bag on the desk and rummages in it, producing a box*) Frank, I got you a present—it isn't much but I thought... (*She gives him a small box*) Here.

*Frank puts on his glasses, gets the scissors out of the pot on the desk, cuts the string and opens the box to reveal an expensive pen*

See what it says—it's engraved.

**Frank** (*reading*) "Must only be used for poetry. By strictest order—Rita"... (*He looks at her*)

**Rita** I thought it'd be like a gentle hint.

**Frank** Gentle?

**Rita** Every time y' try an' write a letter or a note with that pen ... it won't work; you'll read the inscription an' it'll make you feel dead guilty—cos y' not writing poetry. (*She smiles at him*)

**Frank** (*getting up and pecking her on the cheek*) Thank you—Rita. (*He sits down again*)

**Rita** It's a pleasure. Come on. (*She claps her hands*) What are we doin' this term? Let's do a dead good poet. Come on, let's go an' have the tutorial down there.

**Frank** (*appalled*) Down where?

**Rita** (*getting her bag*) Down there—on the grass—come on.

**Frank** On the grass? Nobody sits out there at this time of year.

**Rita** They do—(*looking out of the window*)—there's some of them out there now.

**Frank** Well, they'll have wet bums.

**Rita** What's a wet bum? You can sit on a bench. (*She tries to pull him to his feet*) Come on.

**Frank** (*remaining sitting*) Rita, I absolutely protest.

**Rita** Why?

**Frank** Like Dracula. I have an aversion to sunlight.

**Rita** Tch. (*She sighs*) All right. (*She goes to the window*) Let's open a window.

**Frank** If you must open a window then go on, open it. (*He swivels round to watch her*)

**Rita** (*struggling to open the window*) It won't bleedin' budge.

**Frank** I'm not surprised, my dear. It hasn't been opened for generations.

**Rita** (*abandoning it*) Tch. Y' need air in here, Frank. The room needs airing. (*She goes and opens the door*)

**Frank** This room does not need air, thank you very much.

**Rita** Course it does. A room is like a plant.

**Frank** A room is like a plant?

**Rita** Yeh, it needs air. (*She goes to her chair by the desk and sits*)

**Frank** And water, too, presumably? (*He gets up and closes the door*) If you're going to make an analogy why don't we take it the whole way? Let's get a watering can and water the carpet; bring in two tons of soil and a bag of fertilizer. Maybe we could take cuttings and germinate other little rooms.

**Rita** Go away, you're mental, you are.

**Frank** You said it, distinctly, you said, a room is like a plant.

**Rita** Well!

*There is a pause*

**Frank** Well what?

**Rita** Well, any analogy will break down eventually.

**Frank** Yes. And some will break down sooner than others. (*He smiles, goes to the bookcase and begins searching among the books*) Look, come on... A great poet you wanted—we have one for you.

*Rita sits on the desk watching Frank*

I was going to introduce you to him earlier.

*As he rummages, a book falls to one side revealing a bottle of whisky which
has been hidden behind it*

Now—where is he...?

*Rita goes over and picks the whisky bottle from the shelf*

**Rita**  Are you still on this stuff?
**Frank**  Did I ever say I wasn't?
**Rita**  (*putting the bottle down and moving away*) No. But...
**Frank**  But what?
**Rita**  Why d' y' do it when y've got so much goin' for y', Frank?
**Frank**  It is indeed because I have "so much goin' for me" that I do it. Life
is such a rich and frantic whirl that I need the drink to help me step
delicately through it.
**Rita**  It'll kill y', Frank.
**Frank**  Rita, I thought you weren't interested in reforming me.
**Rita**  I'm not. It's just...
**Frank**  What?
**Rita**  Just that I thought you'd start reforming yourself...
**Frank**  Under your influence?

*She shrugs*

(*He stops searching and turns to face her*) Yes. But Rita—if I repent and
reform, what do I do when your influence is no longer here? What do I do
when, in appalling sobriety, I watch you walk away and disappear, your
influence gone forever?
**Rita**  Who says I'm gonna disappear?
**Frank**  Oh you will, Rita. You've got to. (*He turns back to the shelves*)
**Rita**  Why have I got to? This course could go on for years. An' when I've
got through this one I might even get into the proper university here.
**Frank**  And we'll all live happily ever after? Your going is as inevitable as—
as...
**Rita**  Macbeth?
**Frank**  (*smiling*) As tragedy, yes: but it will not be a tragedy, because I will
be glad to see you go.
**Rita**  Tch. Thank you very much. (*She pauses*) Will y' really?
**Frank**  Be glad to see you go? Well, I certainly don't want to see you stay
in a room like this for the rest of your life. Now. (*He continues searching
for the book*)
**Rita**  (*after a pause*) You can be a real misery sometimes, can't y'? I was dead
happy a minute ago an' then you start an' make me feel like I'm having a
bad night in a mortuary.

*Frank finds the book he has been looking for and moves towards Rita with it*

**Frank** Well, here's something to cheer you up—here's our "dead good" poet—Blake.
**Rita** Blake? William Blake?
**Frank** The man himself. *You* will understand Blake; they overcomplicate him, Rita, but you will understand—you'll love the man.
**Rita** I know.
**Frank** What? (*He opens the book*) Look—look—read this... (*He hands her the book and then goes and sits in the swivel chair*)

*Rita looks at the poem on the page indicated and then looks at Frank*

**Rita** (*reciting from memory*)
    "O Rose, thou art sick!
    The invisible worm
    That flies in the night,
    In the howling storm,

    Has found out thy bed
    Of crimson joy
    And his dark secret love
    Does thy life destroy."
**Frank** You know it!
**Rita** (*laughing*) Yeh. (*She tosses the book on the desk and perches on the bookcase*) We did him at summer school.
**Frank** Blake at summer school? You weren't supposed to do Blake at summer school, were you?
**Rita** Nah. We had this lecturer though, he was a real Blake freak. He was on about it every day. Everythin' he said, honest, everything was related to Blake—he couldn't get his dinner in the refectory without relating it to Blake—Blake and Chips. He was good though. On the last day we brought him a present, an' on it we put that poem, y' know, *The Sick Rose*. But we changed it about a bit; it was—erm——
    "O Rose, thou aren't sick
    Just mangled and dead
    Since the rotten gardener
    Pruned off thy head."
We thought he might be narked but he wasn't, he loved it. He said—what was it? He said, "Parody is merely a compliment masquerading as humour".
**Frank** (*getting up and replacing the book on the shelf*) So ... you've already done Blake? You've covered all the *Songs of Innocence and Experience*?

**Rita** Of course; you don't do Blake without doing innocence and experience, do y'?

**Frank** No. Of course. (*He goes and sits in the swivel chair*)

*Black-out*

   *Rita picks up her bag and shawl and exits*

*Frank is sitting at his desk, marking an essay. Occasionally he makes a tutting sound and scribbles something. There is a knock at the door*

**Frank** Come in.

   *Rita enters, closes the door, goes to the desk and dumps her bag on it. She takes her chair and places it next to Frank and sits down*

**Rita** (*in a peculiar voice*) Hallo, Frank.

**Frank** (*without looking up*) Hallo. Rita, you're late.

**Rita** I know, Frank, I'm terribly sorry. It was unavoidable.

**Frank** (*looking up*) Was it really? What's wrong with your voice?

**Rita** Nothing is wrong with it, Frank. I have merely decided to talk properly. As Trish says there is not a lot of point in discussing beautiful literature in an ugly voice.

**Frank** You haven't got an ugly voice; at least you *didn't* have. Talk properly.

**Rita** I am talking properly. I have to practise constantly, in everyday situations.

**Frank** You mean you're going to talk like that for the rest of this tutorial?

**Rita** Trish says that no matter how difficult I may find it I must persevere.

**Frank** Well, will you kindly tell Trish that I am not giving a tutorial to a parrot.

**Rita** I am not a parrot.

**Frank** (*appealingly*) Rita, stop it!

**Rita** But Frank, I have to persevere in order that I shall.

**Frank** Rita! Just be yourself.

**Rita** (*reverting to her normal voice*) I am being myself. (*She gets up and moves the chair back to its usual place*)

**Frank** What's that?

**Rita** What?

**Frank** On your back.

**Rita** (*reaching up*) Oh—it's grass.

**Frank** Grass?

**Rita** Yeh, I got here early today. I started talking to some students down on the lawn. (*She sits in her usual chair*)

**Frank** You were talking to students—down there?

**Rita** (*laughing*) Don't sound so surprised. I can talk now, y' know, Frank.

**Frank** I'm not surprised. Well! You used to be quite wary of them, didn't you?

**Rita** God knows why. For students they don't half come out with some rubbish, y' know.

**Frank** You're telling me?

**Rita** I only got talking to them in the first place because as I was walking past I heard one of them sayin' as a novel he preferred *Lady Chatterley* to *Sons and Lovers*. I thought, I can keep walkin' and ignore it, or I can put him straight. So I put him straight. I walked over an' said, "Excuse me but I couldn't help overhearin' the rubbish you were spoutin' about Lawrence". Shoulda seen the faces on them, Frank. I said tryin' to compare *Chatterley* with *Sons and Lovers* is like tryin' to compare sparkling wine with champagne. The next thing is there's this heated discussion, with me right in the middle of it.

**Frank** I thought you said the student claimed to "prefer" *Chatterley* as a novel.

**Rita** He did.

**Frank** So he wasn't actually suggesting that it was superior.

**Rita** Not at first—but then he did. He walked right into it…

**Frank** And you finished him off, did you, Rita?

**Rita** Frank, he was asking for it. He was an idiot. His argument just crumbled. It wasn't just me—everyone else agreed with me.

*Frank returns to reading the essay*

There was this really mad one with them; I've only been talkin' to them for five minutes and he's inviting me to go abroad with them all. They're all goin' to the South of France in the Christmas holidays, slummin' it.

**Frank** You can't go.

**Rita** What?

**Frank** You can't go—you've got your exams.

**Rita** My exams are before Christmas.

**Frank** Well—you've got your results to wait for…

**Rita** Tch. I couldn't go anyway.

**Frank** Why? (*He looks at her*)

**Rita** It's all right for them. They *can* just jump into a bleedin' van an' go away. But I can't.

*Frank returns to the essay*

Tiger they call him, he's the mad one. His real name's Tyson but they call him Tiger.

**Frank** (*looking up*) Is there any point me going on with this? (*He points to the essay*)

**Rita** What?

**Frank** Is there much point in working towards an examination if you're going to fall in love and set off for the South of——

**Rita** (*shocked*) What! Fall in love? With who? My God, Frank, I've just been talkin' to some students. I've heard of match-making but this is ridiculous.

**Frank** All right, but please stop burbling on about Mr Tyson.

**Rita** I haven't been burbling on.

*He returns to the essay*

What's it like?

**Frank** Oh—it—erm—wouldn't look out of place with these. (*He places it on top of a pile of other essays on his desk*)

**Rita** Honest?

**Frank** Dead honest.

*Black-out*

*Frank exits*

<h2 style="text-align:center">SCENE 3</h2>

*Rita is sitting in the armchair by the window, reading a heavy tome. There is the sound of muffled oaths from behind the door*

*Frank enters, carrying his briefcase. He is very drunk*

**Frank** Sod them—no, fuck them! Fuck them, eh; Rita. (*He goes to the desk*)

**Rita** Who?

**Frank** You'd tell them, wouldn't you? You'd tell them where to get off. (*He gets a bottle of whisky from his briefcase*)

**Rita** Tell who, Frank?

**Frank** Yes—students—students reported me! (*He goes to the bookcase and puts the whisky on the shelf*) Me! Complained—you know something? They complained and it was the best lecture I've ever given.

**Rita** Were you pissed?

**Frank** Pissed? I was glorious! Fell off the rostrum twice. (*He comes round to the front of the desk*)

**Rita** Will they sack you?

**Frank** (*lying flat on the floor*) The sack? God no; that would involve making a decision. Pissed is all right. To get the sack it'd have to be rape on a grand scale; and not just the students either.

*Rita gets up and moves across to look at him*

That would only amount to a slight misdemeanour. For dismissal it'd have to be nothing less than buggering the bursar... They suggested a sabbatical for a year—or ten... Europe—or America... I suggested that Australia might be more apt—the allusion was lost on them...

**Rita** Tch. Frank, you're mad. Even if y' don't think about yourself, what about the students?

**Frank** What about the students?

**Rita** Well, it's hardly fair on them if their lecturer's so pissed that he's falling off the rostrum. (*She goes to her chair by the desk and replaces the book in her bag*)

**Frank** I might have fallen off, my dear, but I went down talking—and came up talking—never missed a syllable—what have they got to complain about?

**Rita** Maybe they did it for your own good.

**Frank** Or maybe they did it because they're a crowd of mealy-mouthed pricks who wouldn't know a poet if you beat them about the head with one. (*He half sits up*) "Assonance"—I said to them—"Assonance means getting the rhyme wrong..." (*He collapses on the floor again*) They looked at me as though I'd pissed on Wordsworth's tomb.

**Rita** Look, Frank, we'll talk about the Blake essay next week, eh?

**Frank** Where are you going? We've got a tutorial. (*He gets up and staggers towards her*)

**Rita** Frank, you're not in any fit state for a tutorial. I'll leave it with y' an' we can talk about it next week, eh?

**Frank** No—no—you must stay—erm... Watch this—sober? (*He takes a huge breath and pulls himself together*) Sober! Come on...

*He takes hold of Rita and pushes her round the desk and sits her in the swivel chair*

You can't go. I want to talk to you about this. (*He gets her essay and shows it to her*) Rita, what's this?

**Rita** Is there something wrong with it?

**Frank** It's just, look, this passage about *The Blossom*—you seem to assume that the poem is about sexuality.

**Rita** It is!

**Frank** Is it?

**Rita** Well, it's certainly like a richer poem, isn't it? If it's interpreted in that way.

**Frank** Richer? Why richer? We discussed it. The poem is a simple, uncomplicated piece about blossom, as if seen from a child's point of view.

**Rita** (*shrugging*) In one sense. But it's like, like the poem about the rose, isn't it? It becomes a more rewarding poem when you see that it works on a number of levels.

**Frank** Rita, *The Blossom* is a simple, uncomplicated——

**Rita** Yeh, that's what you say, Frank; but Trish and me and some others were talkin' the other night, about Blake, an' what came out of our discussion was that apart from the simple surface value of Blake's poetry there's always a like—erm—erm...

**Frank** Well? Go on...

**Rita** (*managing to*) ...a like vein. Of concealed meaning. I mean if that poem's only about blossom then it's not much of a poem, is it?

**Frank** So? You think it gains from being interpreted in this way?

**Rita** (*slightly defiantly*) Is me essay wrong then, Frank?

**Frank** It's not—not wrong. But I don't like it.

**Rita** You're being subjective.

**Frank** (*half laughing*) Yes—yes, I suppose I am. (*He goes slowly to the chair of the desk and sits down heavily*)

**Rita** If it was in an exam what sort of mark would it get?

**Frank** A good one.

**Rita** Well, what the hell are you sayin' then?

**Frank** (*shrugging*) What I'm saying is that it's up to the minute, quite acceptable, trendy stuff about Blake; but there's nothing of you in there.

**Rita** Or maybe, Frank, y' mean there's nothing of your views in there.

**Frank** (*after a pause*) Maybe that is what I mean.

**Rita** But when I first came to you, Frank, you didn't give me any views. You let me find my own.

**Frank** (*gently*) And your views I still value. But, Rita, these aren't your views.

**Rita** But you told me not to have a view. You told me to be objective, to consult recognized authorities. Well, that's what I've done. I've talked to other people, read other books an' after consultin' a wide variety of opinion I came up with those conclusions.

*He looks at her*

**Frank** (*after a pause*) Yes. All right.

**Rita** (*rattled*) Look, Frank, I don't have to go along with your views on Blake, y' know. I can have a mind of my own, can't I?

**Frank** I sincerely hope so, my dear.

**Rita** And what's that supposed to mean?

**Frank** It means—it means be careful.

*Rita jumps up and moves in towards Frank*

**Rita** (*angrily*) What d' y' mean be careful? I can look after myself. Just 'cos
I'm learnin', just 'cos I can do it now an' read what I wanna read an'
understand without havin' to come runnin' to you every five minutes y'
start tellin' me to be careful. (*She paces about*)
**Frank** Because—because I care for you—I want you to care for yourself.
**Rita** Tch. (*She goes right up to Frank. After a pause*) I—I care for you,
Frank... But you've got to—to leave me alone a bit. I'm not an idiot now,
Frank—I don't need you to hold me hand as much... I can—I can do things
on me own more now... And I am careful. I know what I'm doin'. Just
don't—don't keep treatin' me as though I'm the same as when I first
walked in here. I understand now, Frank; I know the difference between—
between—Thomas Hardy and Rita Mae Brown. An' you're still treating
me as though I'm hung up on *Rubyfruit Jungle*. (*She goes to the swivel
chair and sits*) Just... You understand, don't you, Frank?
**Frank** Entirely, my dear.
**Rita** I'm sorry.
**Frank** Not at all. (*After a pause*) I got round to reading it you know, *Rubyfruit
Jungle*. It's excellent.
**Rita** (*laughing*) Oh, go away, Frank. Of its type it's quite interesting. But it's
hardly excellence.

*Black-out*

*Rita exits*

SCENE 4

*Frank is sitting in the swivel chair*

*Rita enters and goes to the desk*

**Rita** Frank...

*He looks at his watch*

I know I'm late... I'm sorry.

*He gets up and moves away*

Am I too late? We were talkin'. I didn't notice the time.

**Frank** Talking?

**Rita** Yeh. If it'll go in my favour we were talking about Shakespeare.

**Frank** Yes... I'm sure you were.

**Rita** Am I too late then? All right. I'll be on time next week, I promise.

**Frank** Rita. Don't go.

**Rita** No—honestly, Frank—I know I've wasted your time. I'll see y' next week, eh?

**Frank** Rita! Sit down!

*Rita goes to her usual chair and sits*

(*Going to the side of her*) When you were so late I phoned the shop.

**Rita** Which shop?

**Frank** The hairdresser's shop. Where you work. Or, I should say, worked.

**Rita** I haven't worked there for a long time. I work in a bistro now.

**Frank** You didn't tell me.

**Rita** Didn't I? I was telling someone.

**Frank** It wasn't me.

**Rita** Oh. Sorry.

**Frank** (*after a pause*) It struck me that there was a time when you told me everything.

**Rita** I thought I had told you.

**Frank** No. Like a drink?

**Rita** Who cares if I've left hairdressin' to work in a bistro?

**Frank** I care. (*He goes to the bookshelves and takes a bottle from an eye-level shelf*) You don't want a drink? Mind if I do?

**Rita** But why do you care about details like that? It's just boring, insignificant detail.

**Frank** (*getting a mug from the small table*) Oh. Is it?

**Rita** That's why I couldn't stand being in a hairdresser's any longer; boring irrelevant detail all the time, on and on... Well, I'm sorry but I've had enough of that. I don't wanna talk about irrelevant rubbish anymore.

**Frank** And what do you talk about in your bistro? Cheers.

**Rita** Everything.

**Frank** Everything?

**Rita** Yeh.

**Frank** Ah.

**Rita** We talk about what's important, Frank, and we leave out the boring details for those who want them.

**Frank** Is Mr Tyson one of your customers?

**Rita** A lot of the students come in; he's one of them. You're not gonna give me another warning, are y', Frank?

**Frank** Would it do any good?

**Rita** Look, for your information I do find Tiger fascinatin', like I find a lot of the people I mix with fascinating; they're young, and they're passionate about things that matter. They're not trapped—they're too young for that. And I like to be with them.

**Frank** (*moving and keeping his back to her*) Perhaps—perhaps you don't want to waste your time coming here any more?

**Rita** Don't be stupid. I'm sorry I was late. (*After a pause she gets up*) Look, Frank, I've got to go. I'm meeting Trish at seven. We're going to see a production of *The Seagull*.

**Frank** Yes. (*He turns to face her*) Well. When Chekhov calls...

**Rita** Tch.

**Frank** You can hardly bear to spend a moment here, can you?

**Rita** (*moving towards him a little*) That isn't true. It's just that I've got to go to the theatre.

**Frank** And last week you didn't turn up at all. Just a phone call to say that you had to cancel.

**Rita** It's just that—that there's so many things happening now. It's harder.

**Frank** As I said, Rita, if you want to stop com——

**Rita** (*going right up to him*) For God's sake, I don't want to stop coming here. I've got to come here. What about my exam?

**Frank** Oh, I wouldn't worry about that. You'd sail through it anyway. You really don't have to put in the odd appearance out of sentimentality. (*He moves round to the other side of the desk*) I'd rather you spared me that. (*He goes to drink*)

**Rita** If you could stop pouring that junk down your throat in the hope that it'll make you feel like a poet you might be able to talk about things that matter instead of where I do or do not work, an' then it might be worth comin' here.

**Frank** Are you capable of recognizing what does or does not matter, Rita?

**Rita** I understand literary criticism, Frank. When I come here that's what we're supposed to be dealing with.

**Frank** You want literary criticism? (*He looks at her for a moment and then goes to the top drawer of his desk and takes out two slim volumes and some typewritten sheets of poetry and hands them to her*) I want an essay on that lot by next week.

**Rita** What is it?

**Frank** No sentimentality, no subjectivity. Just pure criticism. A critical assessment of a lesser-known English poet. Me.

*Black-out*

*Rita exits*

SCENE 5

*Frank is sitting in a chair by the window desk with a mug in his hand and a bottle of whisky on the desk in front of him, listening to the radio. There is a knock at the door*

**Frank** Come in.

*Rita enters and goes to the swivel chair behind Frank's desk*

(*Getting up and switching off the radio*) What the—what the hell are you doing here? I'm not seeing you till next week.

**Rita** Are you sober? Are you?

**Frank** If you mean am I still this side of reasonable comprehension, then yes.

**Rita** (*going and standing next to him*) Because I want you to hear this when you're sober. (*She produces his poems*) These are brilliant. Frank, you've got to start writing again. (*She goes to the swivel chair and sits*) This is brilliant. They're witty. They're profound. Full of style.

**Frank** (*going to the small table and putting down his mug*) Ah ... tell me again, and again.

**Rita** They are, Frank. It isn't only me who thinks so. Me an' Trish sat up last night and read them. She agrees with me. Why did you stop writing? Why did you stop writing when you can produce work like this? We stayed up most of the night, just talking about it. At first we just saw it as contemporary poetry in its own right, you know, as somethin' particular to this century but look, Frank, what makes it more—more... What did Trish say—? More resonant than—purely contemperory poetry is that you can see in it a direct line through to nineteenth-century traditions of—of like wit an' classical allusion.

**Frank** (*going to the chair of the desk and standing by the side of it*) Er—that's erm—that's marvellous, Rita. How fortunate I didn't let you see it earlier. Just think if I'd let you see it when you first came here.

**Rita** I know... I wouldn't have understood it, Frank.

**Frank** You would have thrown it across the room and dismissed it as a heap of shit, wouldn't you?

**Rita** (*laughing*) I know... But I couldn't have understood it then, Frank, because I wouldn't have been able to recognize and understand the allusions.

**Frank** Oh, I've done a fine job on you, haven't I?

**Rita** It's true, Frank. I can see now.

**Frank** You know, Rita, I think—I think that like you I shall change my name; from now on I shall insist upon being known as Mary, Mary Shelley—do you understand that allusion, Rita?

**Rita** What?

**Frank** She wrote a little Gothic number called *Frankenstein*.

**Rita** So?

**Frank** This—(*picking up his poetry and moving round to Rita*)—this clever, pyrotechnical pile of self-conscious allusion is worthless, talentless, shit and could be recognized as such by anyone with a shred of common sense. It's the sort of thing that gives publishing a bad name. Wit? You'll find more wit in the telephone book, and, probably, more insight. Its one advantage over the telephone directory is that it's easier to rip. (*He rips the poems up and throws the pieces on to the desk*) It is pretentious, characterless and without style.

**Rita** It's not.

**Frank** Oh, I don't expect you to believe me, Rita; you recognize the hallmark of literature now, don't you? (*In a final gesture he throws a handful of the ripped pieces into the air and then goes to the chair and sits*) Why don't you just go away? I don't think I can bear it any longer.

**Rita** Can't bear what, Frank?

**Frank** You, my dear—you...

**Rita** I'll tell you what you can't bear, Mr Self-Pitying-Piss Artist; what you can't bear is that I am educated now. What's up, Frank, don't y' like me now that the little girl's grown up, now that y' can no longer bounce me on daddy's knee an' watch me stare back in wide-eyed wonder at everything he has to say? I'm educated, I've got what you have an' y' don't like it because you'd rather see me as the peasant I once was; you're like the rest of them—you like to keep your natives thick, because that way they still look charming and delightful. I don't need you. (*She gets up and picking her bag moves away from the desk in the direction of the door*) I know what clothes to wear, what wine to buy, what plays to see, what papers and books to read. I can do without you.

**Frank** Is that all you wanted? Have you come all this way for so very, very little?

**Rita** Oh, it's little to you, isn't it? It's little to you who squanders every opportunity and mocks and takes it for granted.

**Frank** Found a culture have you, Rita? Found a better song to sing, have you? No—you've found a different song, that's all—and on your lips it's shrill and hollow and tuneless. Oh, Rita, Rita...

**Rita** Rita? (*She laughs*) Rita? Nobody calls me Rita but you. I dropped that pretentious crap as soon as I saw it for what it was. You stupid... Nobody calls me Rita.

**Frank** What is it now then? Virginia?

*Rita exits, slamming the door*

Or Charlotte? Or Jane? Or Emily? Virginia?

*Black-out*


SCENE 6

*Frank talking into the phone. He is leaning against the bookshelf. He is very drunk*

**Frank** Yes... I think she works there... Rita White. No, no. Sorry ... erm. What is it? Susan White? No? Thank you... Thanks. (*He dials another number*) Yes... Erm... Trish, is it? ... Erm, yes, I'm a friend of Rita's... I'm sorry, Susan. ... Yes ... could you just say that—erm—I've ... it's—erm—Frank here... her tutor... Yes... well, could you tell her I've entered her for her examination... Yes, you see she doesn't know the details ... time and where the exam is being held... Could you tell her to call in? ... Please... Yes. ... Thank you.

*The Lights fade to Black-out*


SCENE 7

*Rita enters and shuts the door. She is wrapped in a large winter coat. She lights a cigarette and moves across to a filing cabinet and places a Christmas card with the others already there. She throws the envelope in the waste-bin and opens the door, revealing Frank with a couple of tea chests either side of him*

*He is taken aback seeing her, and then he gathers himself and picking up one of the chests, enters the room*

*Rita goes out to the corridor and brings in the other chest. Frank gets the chair from the end of his desk and places it by the bookcase. He stands on it and begins taking down the books from the shelves and putting them into the chests. Rita watches him but he continues as if she is not there*

**Rita** Merry Christmas, Frank. Have they sacked y'?
**Frank** Not quite.
**Rita** Well, why y'—packing your books away?
**Frank** Australia. (*He pauses*) Some weeks ago—made rather a night of it.
**Rita** Did y' bugger the bursar?

**Frank** Metaphorically. And as it was metaphorical the sentence was reduced from the sack to two years in Australia. Hardly a reduction in sentence really—but...

**Rita** What did Julia say?

**Frank** *Bon voyage.*

**Rita** She's not goin' with y'?

*Frank shakes his head. Rita begins helping him take down the books from the shelves and putting them in the chests*

What y' gonna do?

**Frank** What do you think I'll do. Aussie? It's a paradise for the likes of me.

**Rita** Tch. Come on, Frank...

**Frank** It is. Didn't you know the Australians named their favourite drink after a literary figure? Forster's Lager they call it. Of course they get the spelling wrong—rather like you once did!

**Rita** Be serious.

**Frank** For God's sake, why did you come back here?

**Rita** I came to tell you you're a good teacher. *(After a pause)* Thanks for enterin' me for the exam.

**Frank** That's all right. I know how much it had come to mean to you.

*Rita perches on the small table while Frank continues to take books from the upper shelves*

**Rita** You didn't want me to take it, did y'? Eh? You woulda loved it if I'd written "Frank knows all the answers", across me paper, wouldn't y'? I nearly did an' all. When the invigilator said, "Begin", I turned over me paper with the rest of them, and while they were all scribbling away against the clock, I just sat there, lookin' at the first question. Y' know what it was, Frank? "Suggest ways in which one might cope with some of the staging difficulties in a production of *Peer Gynt*".

*Frank gets down, sits on the chair and continues to pack the books*

**Frank** Well, you should have had no trouble with that.

**Rita** I did though. I just sat lookin' at the paper an' thinkin' about what you'd said. I tried to ignore it, to pretend that you were wrong. You think you gave me nothing; did nothing for me. You think I just ended up with a load of quotes an' empty phrases; an' I did. But that wasn't your doin'. I was so hungry. I wanted it all so much that I didn't want it to be questioned. I told y' I was stupid. It's like Trish, y' know me flatmate. I thought she was so cool an' together—I came home the other night an' she'd tried to top herself. What's all that about? She spends half her life eatin' wholefoods an' health foods to make her live longer an' the other half tryin' to kill herself. (*She pauses*) I sat lookin' at the question, an' thinkin' about it all. Then I picked up me pen an' started.

**Frank** And you wrote, "Do it on the radio"?

**Rita** I could have done. An' you'd have been proud of me if I'd done that an' rushed back to tell you—wouldn't y'? But I chose not to. I had a choice. I did the exam.

**Frank** I know. A good pass as well.

**Rita** Yeh. An' it might be worthless in the end. But I had a choice. I chose, me. Because of what you'd given me. I had a choice. I wanted to come back an' tell y' that. That y' a good teacher.

**Frank** (*stopping working and looking at her*) You know—erm—I hear very good things about Australia. The thing is, why don't you—come as well?

**Rita** Isn't that called jumpin' a sinkin' ship?

**Frank** So what? Do you really think there's any chance of keeping it afloat?

*She looks at him and then at the shelves*

**Rita** (*seeing the empty whisky bottles*) 'Ey, Frank, what's it like havin' your own bottle bank?

**Frank** (*smiling*) You're being evasive.

**Rita** (*going and sitting on a tea chest*) I know. Tiger's asked me to go down to France with his mob.

**Frank** Will you?

**Rita** I dunno. He's a bit of a wanker really. But I've never been to France. An' me mother's invited me to hers for Christmas.

**Frank** What are you going to do?

**Rita** I dunno. I might go to France. I might go to me mother's. I might even have a baby. I dunno. I'll make a decision, I'll choose. I dunno.

*Frank has found a package hidden behind some of the books. He takes it down*

**Frank** Whatever you do, you might as well take this...

**Rita** What?

**Frank** (*handing it to her*) It's erm—well, it's er—it's a dress really. I brought it some time ago—for erm—for an educated woman friend—of mine...

*Rita takes the dress from the bag*

I erm—don't—know if it fits, I was rather pissed when I brought it...

**Rita** An educated woman, Frank? An' this is what you call a scholarly neckline?

**Frank** When choosing it I put rather more emphasis on the word woman than
  the word educated.
**Rita** All I've ever done is take from you. I've never given anything.
**Frank** That's not true, you've——
**Rita** It is true. I never thought there was anythin' I could give you. But there
  is. Come here, Frank...
**Frank** What?
**Rita** Come here... (*She pulls out a chair*) Sit on that...

*Frank is bewildered*

  Sit...

*Frank sits and Rita, eventually finding a pair of scissors on the desk; waves
them in the air*

  I'm gonna take ten years off you... (*She goes across to him and begins to
  cut his hair*)

*Black-out*

CURTAIN

# FURNITURE AND PROPERTY LIST

Further dressing may be added at the director's discretion

## ACT I

### SCENE 1

*On stage*: **Frank**'s desk. *On it*: pot containing scissors, pens, pencils, etc.; various books, essays and papers including **Rita**'s admission paper, desk lamp
Swivel chair
Chair at **Frank**'s desk
Waste-paper basket
Filing cabinet. *On it*: telephone, desk lamp
Bookcases/shelves containing books and 2 bottles of whisky hidden behind, one almost empty
Window-desk. *On it*: radio, portable typewriter, Anglepoise lamp
Small table covered with various books and papers
Ashtray
Armchair
Print of nude religious scene
Empty mug

*Off stage*: Bag containing copy of *Rubyfruit Jungle*, packet of cigarettes, lighter (**Rita**)

*Personal*: **Frank**: wristwatch, pair of glasses (worn throughout)

### SCENE 2

*Re-set*: Bottle of whisky
Mug

*Off stage*: Small can of oil, bag containing pen and essay papers (**Rita**)

### SCENE 3

*Strike*: **Rita**'s bag and can of oil

*Off stage*:   Bag containing cigarettes and lighter (**Rita**)

<h3 style="text-align:center">SCENE 4</h3>

*Off stage*:   Bag (**Rita**)

<h3 style="text-align:center">SCENE 5</h3>

*Off stage*:   Briefcase containing lunch and copy of *Rubyfruit Jungle* (**Frank**)
               Bag (**Rita**)

<h3 style="text-align:center">SCENE 6</h3>

*Strike*:      **Frank**'s lunch

<h3 style="text-align:center">SCENE 7</h3>

*Off stage*:   Large holdall (**Rita**)

<h2 style="text-align:center">ACT II</h2>

<h3 style="text-align:center">SCENE 1</h3>

*Strike*:      **Rita**'s holdall

*Set*:         Paper in typewriter
               Lit cigarette
               Carton containing packets of *Gauloise* cigarettes
               Lighter
               Mug

*Off stage*:   Bag. *In it*: gift-wrapped box containing expensive pen (**Rita**)

*Personal*:    **Rita:** shawl

<h3 style="text-align:center">SCENE 2</h3>

*Off stage*:   Bag (**Rita**)

<h3 style="text-align:center">SCENE 3</h3>

*Set*:         Heavy tome
               **Rita**'s essay

*Off stage*:   Briefcase containing bottle of whisky (**Frank**)

SCENE 4

*On stage*:   Whisky bottle on eye-level shelf
Mug on small table
2 slim volumes and typewritten sheets of poetry in top drawer of
Frank's desk

*Off stage*:   Bag (**Rita**)

SCENE 5

*Re-set*:   Mug and bottle of whisky on window desk

*Off stage*:   Bag containing **Frank**'s poetry (**Rita**)

SCENE 6

*Strike*:   Mug and bottle of whisky from window desk

SCENE 7

*Set*:   Christmas cards on filing cabinet
Paper bag containing dress behind books on shelf

*Off stage*:   Bag containing cigarettes and lighter, Christmas card in envelope
(**Rita**)
2 tea chests (**Frank**)

# LIGHTING PLOT

Practical fittings required: 2 desk lamps, picture light, pendant light, standard lamp
1 interior. The same throughout

ACT I, Scene 1

*To open*:    Full general lighting, Frank's desk lamp on, evening lighting outside
window

| | | |
|---|---|---|
| *Cue* 1 | **Frank** switches picture light on<br>*Snap on picture light* | (Page 3) |
| *Cue* 2 | **Frank** switches off picture light<br>*Snap off picture light* | (Page 3) |
| *Cue* 3 | **Rita** exits<br>*Black-out* | (Page 12) |

ACT I, Scene 2

*To open*:    Dim lighting, evening effect through window. Desk light on

| | | |
|---|---|---|
| *Cue* 4 | **Frank** switches on light at door<br>*Bring up full lighting* | (Page 12) |
| *Cue* 5 | **Frank** switches off desk light<br>*Snap off desk light* | (Page 18) |
| *Cue* 6 | **Rita**: "…was a frustrated electrician?"<br>*Black-out* | (Page 19) |

ACT I, SCENE 3

*To open*:    Full general lighting

*Cue* 7       **Frank** switches desk light on                (Page 21)
              *Snap on desk light*

*Cue* 8       **Rita** switches desk light off               (Page 23)
              *Snap off desk light*

*Cue* 9       **Frank** and a beaming **Rita** look at each other   (Page 23)
              *Black-out*


ACT I, SCENE 4

*To open*:    Full general interior lighting; desk lamps & standard lamp on; evening
              effect through window

*Cue* 10      **Frank** switches off the desk lamp          (Page 28)
              *Snap off desk lamp*

*Cue* 11      **Frank** switches off standard lamp          (Page 28)
              *Snap off standard lamp*

*Cue* 12      **Frank** and **Rita** exit                   (Page 28)
              *Black-out*


ACT I, SCENE 5

*To open*:    Full general lighting, daylight through window

*Cue* 13      **Rita**: "What shall I wear?"                (Page 31)
              *Black-out*


ACT I, SCENE 6

*To open*:    Full general lighting, daylight through window

*Cue* 14      **Rita**: "And that's why I'm staying."       (Page 33)
              *Black-out*

ACT I, SCENE 7

*To open*:   Full general lighting, daylight through window

*Cue* 15     **Rita** sits                                   (Page 35)
             *Black-out*


ACT II, SCENE 1

*To open*:   Full general lighting, daylight through window

*Cue* 16     **Frank** sits in swivel chair                 (Page 42)
             *Black-out*


ACT II, SCENE 2

*To open*:   Full general lighting, daylight through window

*Cue* 17     **Frank**: "Dead honest."                      (Page 44)
             *Black-out*


ACT II, SCENE 3

*To open*:   Full general lighting, daylight through window

*Cue* 18     **Rita**: "But it's hardly excellence."         (Page 47)
             *Black-out*


ACT II, SCENE 4

*To open*:   Full general lighting, daylight through window

*Cue* 19     **Frank**: "...a lesser-known English poet. Me." (Page 49)
             *Black-out*

ACT II, SCENE 5

*To open*:   Full general lighting, daylight through window

*Cue* 20     **Frank**: "Or Emily? Virginia?"          (Page 52)
             *Black-out*

ACT II, SCENE 6

*To open*:   Full general lighting, daylight through window

*Cue* 21     **Frank**: "Thank you."                  (Page 52)
             *Fade lights to black-out*

ACT II, SCENE 7

*To open*:   Full general lighting, daylight through window

*Cue* 22     **Rita** starts to cut **Frank**'s hair   (Page 55)
             *Black-out*

# EFFECTS PLOT

## ACT I

*Cue* 1    **Frank** raises the mug to drink                (Page 1)
          *Phone rings*

*Cue* 2    **Frank** switches on the radio                  (Page 28)
          *Bring up Radio Four weather forecast before*
             The World at One

*Cue* 3    **Frank** switches the radio off                 (Page 28)
          *Snap off radio effect*

## ACT II

*Cue* 4    As Scene 5 opens                                 (Page 50)
          *Radio effect*

*Cue* 5    **Frank** switches the radio off                 (Page 50)
          *Snap off radio effect*

MADE AND PRINTED IN GREAT BRITAIN BY
LATIMER TREND & COMPANY LTD PLYMOUTH
MADE IN ENGLAND

CPSIA information can be obtained at www.ICGtesting.com
Printed in the USA
LVOW07s0145040816

498999LV00013B/77/P